PREACH THE WORD

Preach the Word

Homilies on the Sundays and Feasts of
the Extraordinary Form of the Roman Rite

KENNETH BAKER, SJ

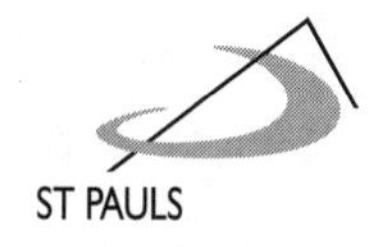

Library of Congress Cataloging-in-Publication Data

Baker, Kenneth.
Preach the word : homilies on the Sundays and feasts of the extraordinary form of the Roman rite / Kenneth Baker.
p. cm.
ISBN 978-0-8189-1314-3
1. Catholic Church—Sermons. I. Title.
BX1756.B325P74 2010
252'.02—dc22
2010016825

Produced and designed in the United States of America by the Fathers and Brothers of the Society of St. Paul, 2187 Victory Boulevard, Staten Island, New York 10314-6603 as part of their communications apostolate.

ISBN 10: 0-8189-1314-2
ISBN 13: 978-0-8189-1314-3

Printing Information:

Current Printing - first digit 1 2 3 4 5 6 7 8 9 10

Year of Current Printing - first year shown
2010 2011 2012 2013 2014 2015 2016 2017 2018 2019

TABLE OF CONTENTS

INTRODUCTION

There are dozens of books of sample homilies for the *Novus Ordo* Lectionary, but I am not aware of any recent collections of homilies for the 1962 Latin *Roman Missal*, now known as the Extraordinary Form of the Roman Rite.

I was ordained in the old rite, but changed to the *Novus Ordo* Mass in 1970, since I was told that, in obedience to the Holy Father, I should start offering Mass in English and to take part in concelebrations. In 1988 I was asked to offer a traditional Latin Mass for a group in New York City who had received permission for it from Cardinal John J. O'Connor. I accepted their offer and began once again, occasionally, to celebrate Mass in Latin. In 1995 I was invited to assist the priests of the Fraternity of St. Peter in New Jersey who celebrate Mass exclusively in Latin according to the 1962 Missal. So I moved into their rectory and have been with them and assisting them for fourteen years. My status there is that I am "in residence," since I am not a member of the staff. For fourteen years now I have been offering the traditional Latin Mass at Our Lady of Fatima Chapel in Pequannock every Sunday at 7 a.m.

Over the years I have accumulated many notes on the Mass for every Sunday of the year and for every feast day. Recently it occurred to me that a collection of homilies for the Extraordinary Form of the Roman Rite might be helpful to priests who have to preach at the Masses and also for members of the faithful who attend the Latin Mass. Their numbers are growing every year, especially since the appearance of the motu proprio issued by Pope Benedict XVI in July 2007, *Summorum Pontificum*.

Accordingly, I have written a homily for each Sunday of the year, for the Holy Days of obligation, and for the First Class feasts that replace the Sunday Mass when that day falls on a Sunday. The total number comes to 75 homilies. Their length is about 1,000 words each. When I preached these homilies the length was about 13 minutes, including the time required to read the Epistle and Gospel for the day.

Every priest has certain themes and ideas that are dear to him and that he stresses in his homilies or sermons. I have noted that also in the sermons of the greatest preacher of our time, Archbishop Fulton J. Sheen. In preaching the Gospel of Jesus Christ, the points that I stress are Baptism, Penance, the Holy Sacrifice of the Mass, sanctifying grace, divine sonship, the will of God, sin and repentance, avoiding the near occasions of sin, faith, hope, Mary the Mother of God, obedience to the Magisterium of the Church, prayer and eternal life. Where it fits in, I have tried to include some of the basic truths taught in the *Catechism of the Catholic Church*.

This book is not intended to be read as one would read a book on some aspect of theology. It is rather a reference book to keep handy when a priest is looking for a few ideas for the homily he must preach at the next Sunday Mass according to the 1962 Roman Rite. I hope and pray that it will be of some assistance to priests, and also to members of the laity who follow the Mass closely in their hand missal. These homilies should help the attentive reader to hear God's word coming to him through the Sunday liturgy.

Kenneth Baker, S.J.
Presentation of the Lord
February 2, 2010

PREACH THE WORD

FIRST SUNDAY OF ADVENT

Readings: Romans 13:11-14; Luke 21:25-33

Prepare Yourself for the Coming of the Lord

The season before Christmas is called "Advent," a word which means "Coming." During this time the Church calls on us to prepare ourselves for the celebration of the feast of Christmas when God became man as a little child in Bethlehem. The time of Advent is four weeks of spiritual preparation for the coming of our Savior.

During Advent we celebrate three comings of Jesus Christ: (1) In love and humility at Bethlehem 2000 years ago; (2) in grace in the sacraments now; (3) in power and glory at the end of the world. During this time the Church urges us to pray more fervently, to repent for our sins and to do some penance, to cleanse ourselves so that we will be more receptive of his coming. This preparation should be both internal and external, but primarily internal. The result of his coming is his presence in our souls by grace which effects an intimate union with us in knowledge and love.

Preparing ourselves for Christmas is like preparing our home to receive guests. Just as we prepare carefully for guests who will come for a Thanksgiving dinner, so also the Church urges us to prepare our souls for the coming of Christ. During Advent we prepare for his coming to us with his grace, we prepare for our own death when he will judge us, and we prepare for Jesus' Second Coming at the end of the world when he will appear in glory as both our Savior and our Judge.

Last Sunday, which was the 24th Sunday after Pentecost and the last Sunday of the liturgical year, we read from St. Matthew's Gospel in Chapter 24 about the Second Coming of Christ, the end of the world and the final or General Judgment. There Jesus revealed certain signs of the end: persecutions, turmoil among nations, disruption of nature in the heavens, and the coming of the Son of Man on the clouds "with great power and majesty" to judge all mankind.

Some of that is repeated today, with emphasis on the Second Coming of Christ. In his First Coming at Bethlehem he came in humility and meekness and remains with us in a hidden way in his Church, especially in the sacraments. In his Second Coming he will come with power. The Father has appointed him as our Judge – he has the power to send us to Heaven or to hell, depending on our merits.

Notice the stark contrast: In Bethlehem he comes as a loving, helpless infant Savior; at the end he is the awesome Avenger of man's sins and Rewarder of good deeds. Why does the Church present such a view to us today – two events that are so different?

By having us think of Jesus as our future Judge, the Church wishes to stir up a holy and salutary fear that will turn us from sin and help us prepare our hearts as a worthy home for him. In divine things, fear prepares the way for love, and we better appreciate our redemption when we consider the fate from which redemption is intended to save us, namely, eternal loss of God and damnation, which means everlasting misery.

At the beginning of Advent the thought of judgment is salutary because it restrains us from the commission of sin. Note what the wise man says in Ecclesiastes 7:40: "In all thy works, remember thy last end, and thou shalt never sin." The thought of judgment and final accounting for our lives spurs us on to the practice of the highest virtue, to prayer and good works. St. Paul refers to this in today's Epistle when he speaks about the contrast between darkness and light: "Let us walk becomingly as in the day.... Put on the Lord Jesus Christ"; "put on" here means to imitate him and to love him. Now God gives us the time to do that.

Time, just like our life, is a gift from God. We should use it wisely to work out our salvation in fear and trembling, as St. Paul says. For, our eternal destiny depends on how we use our time. When we die the time of merit in the eyes of God comes to a close.

Time is a type of motion; it has a beginning, middle and end. God gives each one of us time to become a saint. The length of man's life is threescore and ten years – and 80 years for those who are strong according to Psalm 90:10. For us eternity has a beginning when God created us, but it has no end. We begin our lives in time, but we end them in eternity – either in perfect happiness or perfect misery – forever. God is eternal by his essence and time reaches its purpose and perfection in eternity.

In the first chapter of the Book of Ecclesiastes the wise man tells us that "The fear of the Lord is the beginning of wisdom." This fear means awe, reverence and respect for God. Such fear is called "filial fear"; it is the fear a son has of not offending his father, rather than the servile fear of a slave. It helps us to keep our eyes focused on our last end. It is not so much a fear of punishment as it is a fear of sin and our own weakness. With the help of filial fear we will be able to overcome temptations, which all are subject to, to reject sin and to practice virtue – especially love of God and love of neighbor.

Let us pray today that Christ will come into our hearts in a more intimate way during this Advent so that we may be prepared to meet him with confidence when he comes – and he may come to some of us sooner than we think. Advent is also a time to make a good confession if you have not done so recently.

The Lord has come with love at Bethlehem, he is coming with his grace in the sacraments, and he will come again in glory and power. We need to thank him, to welcome him, and to prepare for him. The beautiful season of Advent helps us to do all three. God bless you.

SECOND SUNDAY OF ADVENT

Readings: Romans 15:4-13; Matthew 11:2-10

The God of Hope

As we saw last Sunday, in Advent we celebrate the three comings of the Lord: He has come at Bethlehem, He is coming now in the sacraments, and He will come again in glory at the end of the world. Advent is a time of hope, expectation and joy because the Lord is near. Our hope is in the Lord who comes to bring us salvation from our sins and eternal life. Advent is also a time to prepare our hearts for the coming of Christ. I would like to call your attention to the words in the Post Communion prayer for today: "Teach us to despise (= consider of less value) the things of earth, and to yearn for the things of Heaven."

John the Baptist, who is featured in today's Gospel reading, is a prime example of that because he led a very austere life in the wilderness preparing himself and others for the coming of the Messiah and the Kingdom of God. The Old Testament gives utterance to the promise of the coming Messiah or king; the fulfillment of that promise is found in Jesus Christ in the New Testament. There are explicit references in Isaiah and Zechariah. As an example, we read in Malachi 3:1: "Behold, I send my messenger to prepare the way before us." But John is more than a prophet – they spoke about the future – but he points out the Messiah and calls him "the Lamb of God." He is greater than all the prophets before him, but the least in the Kingdom of God is greater than he because of sanctifying grace given to us by Jesus Christ which makes us members of his Church which is his body.

The main theme of this Mass is summarized by St. Paul in the Epistle: "Now may the God of hope fill you with all joy and peace in believing, that you may abound in hope and in the power of the Holy Spirit" (Romans 15:3). Also, he refers to Isaiah 11:10 when he says, "In him the Gentiles shall hope."

Hope is a beautiful virtue and word – one of the most positive words in the English language. Here is a good definition: "Hope is the theological virtue infused by God into the will, by which we trust with complete certitude in the attainment of eternal life and the means necessary for reaching it, assisted by the omnipotent help of God." (See J. Aumann, *Spiritual Theology*, p. 258.)

Hope on the natural level means that we expect to achieve something in the future as a result of our own efforts or good fortune. The hope we are talking about here is supernatural hope. The primary object of supernatural hope is to attain eternal beatitude, which is Heaven or the face to face vision of God. The secondary object includes the means to attain the end, such as prayer, the sacrament, grace, the Bible. Supernatural hope tends to its object with absolute certitude because it flows from faith which is certain above all things and because it is based on the word of God which cannot deceive. The goods of this life fall under the secondary object, but only insofar as they help us to achieve salvation.

The two major failings or sins against hope are presumption and despair. We have an abundance of both of these in our post-Christian culture. Presumption means taking God for granted and not using the normal means to be saved. This includes those people who sin regularly but think they will go to Heaven just the same since, as they say, "God is a good guy and he will not send anyone to hell – if there is a hell." Despair means that one abandons all hope of salvation. For example, one might think his sins are so great that God could not forgive them so he refuses to repent and ask for forgiveness – Judas Iscariot would be a case in point.

Christian hope and joy are a consequence of faith and love of Jesus Christ. What is the basic reason for the great joy of Christmas? It is the hope of eternal salvation merited by Jesus and offered to all. Today's Introit is a sign of this: "People of Sion, behold, the Lord shall come to save the nations" (Isaiah 30:20).

We are surrounded with a wholly secular culture and earthly view of the "holidays" at the end of December. As Catholics we should avoid that mentality. Christmas means that we are celebrating the coming, the birth of our Savior. He offers us permanent, eternal happiness. Don't leave Christ out of your Christmas.

When others say to you "Happy Holidays" or "Season's Greetings," look them in the eye and, with a smile, wish them a "Happy Christmas" or "Merry Christmas." Above all, be filled with hope and joy because God is coming to save us. We rejoice not because of the eating, drinking and exchange of gifts. These should be the "external" signs of our "interior joy" because of the birth of our Savior. Let us make the words of St. Paul our own: "Now may the God of hope fill you with all joy and peace in believing, that you may abound in hope and in the power of the Holy Spirit." God bless you.

THIRD SUNDAY OF ADVENT

Readings: Philippians 4:4-7; John 1:19-28

Rejoice! The Lord Is Near

In one sense, the approach of Christmas means that the Lord is near. The advent or coming of God, for those who desire him, causes joy in our hearts. In the third Sunday of Advent the Church stresses joy in the liturgy. The first word of the Introit in Latin is *Gaudete* which means "Rejoice." There St. Paul tells the Philippians: "Rejoice in the Lord always, again I say, rejoice! The Lord is near."

There is a close connection, therefore, between joy and the presence of God, because joy is the emotion that fills the heart at the anticipation and possession of any desired good. God is the supreme, infinite good – both in himself and also for finite, created souls, namely, us. The Psalms and prophets in the Old Testament are full of calls to joy, to rejoice, to clap hands for joy at the presence of God – in his mighty works or miracles and in the gifts of nature he gives us. The Church applies all of these to the coming of Jesus at Bethlehem.

Joy is an emotion that results from the anticipation or possession of a known good. Joy can only be in a spiritual being with intellect and will – angels and men. It assumes the ability to look into the future which only a spiritual being can do. Animals cannot rejoice in anything because they are totally material. A cow can be contented with lots of green grass or corn, but it is not full of joy.

The theme for today's Mass is "Rejoice, for the Lord is near." He is coming. He brings us redemption from our sins. He brings us hope because he will save us from death and open the gates of Heaven to us. Also, we rejoice because he is near us in the tabernacle and in our souls by his grace.

Last week we encountered John the Baptist. John is a witness to the light and truth of God so that through him men might believe. John is not the light (as some thought at the time), but only a witness to the Light or Truth. Jesus is the true Light who was with God in the beginning: "In the beginning was the word, and the word was with God...."

The men sent by the Pharisees to quiz him do not ask him what he is doing, but "Who are you?" That is, are you the Messiah? Are you Elijah returned to earth? Are you the prophet mentioned in Deuteronomy 18:15? John's answer is a resounding NO. He says he is the voice of one crying in the wilderness "Make straight the way of the Lord" (quoting Isaiah 40:3). In other words, his role is to point out the Messiah and then withdraw from the stage. He is not the Messiah or Elijah or the prophet.

John points out Jesus as the Messiah not just for the people of that time, but also for us. And note his poverty and humility. He lives in the wilderness, as Elijah did, and he wears rough clothing. There is nothing soft about this man. In reference to Jesus John says that "He must increase and

I must decrease." "I am not worthy to loosen the strap of his sandal" – which, at the time, was the duty of slaves.

John baptizes only with water for repentance and the forgiveness of sins. But he is preparing us for the coming of Christ. Jesus baptizes with water and the Holy Spirit who gives us divine grace and rebirth as children of God and heirs of Heaven.

Since the precursor is there, the Messiah must be near – and he is. He is Jesus of Nazareth who is beginning his public life of preaching and healing and establishing the kingdom of God. But he is not yet known, so John says: "There is one among you whom you do not recognize" – namely Jesus. How true that is even in the Church today for many lazy and faithless Catholics who are Catholic in name only.

The presence of the Messiah and Savior is cause for joy in our hearts, for he is the fulfillment of all the prophecies of the Old Testament. In Him we have everything we need, for God alone suffices to satisfy all our needs. He is the only one who can do it.

Conclusion

Joy is one of the fruits of the Holy Spirit as listed by Paul in Galatians 5:22. It flows from faith and the seven Gifts of the Holy Spirit. It also accompanies the eight Beatitudes. Joy in the Lord is not lost in trials and sufferings, and it should not be confused with pleasure and "having a good time." For example, the Apostles "rejoiced" that they were able to suffer something for Jesus when they were scourged for preaching the Gospel (Acts 5:41).

In the Beatitudes Jesus tells us that joy for the Christian flows from things that are diametrically opposed to what the world esteems: "Blessed are the poor.... Blessed are the meek.... Blessed are those who mourn.... Blessed are the pure of heart.... Blessed are those who suffer persecution.... Rejoice and be glad for your reward will be great in Heaven"

(Matthew 5:11-12) – for you are then more like Jesus who suffered such things for you.

The advent of God, for those who seek him, is a cause of great joy. Let us beg the Lord today to come into our hearts this Christmas more than ever before and fill our hearts with joy. Then with St. Paul we can sing today's Antiphon: "Rejoice in the Lord always; again I say, 'Rejoice,' because the Lord is near."

Jesus is near us in his grace, near us in the tabernacle on the altar, near us in judgment when we meet him face to face after this life in our particular judgment. In Advent we celebrate his coming to us in all these ways.

FOURTH SUNDAY OF ADVENT

Readings: 1 Corinthians 4:1-5; Luke 3:1-6

John the Precursor

The role of St. John the Baptist in announcing the coming of the Messiah is so important that he is featured in the Sunday Gospel of Advent three weeks in a row. He is the one chosen by God to point out the Messiah. He is the greatest of the prophets and he is the bridge between the Old Testament and the New Testament. Notice the majestic introduction Luke gives to John. He situates him historically in time and place. Our Catholic faith, therefore, is based on real historical events and persons. It is not just a philosophy or human invention like Buddhism, Hinduism, Confucianism and Islam.

John was specially chosen by God, like Abraham, Moses and Mary, for a definite task in salvation history. He was sanctified in his mother's womb before he was born. As an adult, he lived in the wilderness of Judea near the Dead Sea and the Jordan River – a very desolate area. He lived an austere life: no home, no wife, no children, and no possessions. His one concern was the service of God and the things of God. Accordingly, John lived a life of solitude, silence, prayer and study of Holy Scripture. His diet was locusts and wild honey and he wore rough camel skin for clothing like the prophet Elijah. He was a strong, rugged man with a mission.

St. Luke tells us that the word of God came to him. This means that God revealed himself to John and sent him on a mission to preach penance for the forgiveness of sins. So he was a prophet like Amos, Isaiah and Ezekiel. His message was one of prayer and penance, very similar to Our Blessed Mother's requests at Lourdes and Fatima.

Because of the sin of Adam and our own personal sins, we need God's forgiveness and grace. How do we achieve that? We achieve it:

1) By telling God we are sorry for our sins, by acts of humility, by acts of penance;
2) John baptized for the forgiveness of sins. His baptism was an external rite used to stir up internal acts of sorrow;
3) John gave good example: He led a penitential life totally dedicated to God.

John quoted Isaiah 40:3 to prove that he was the precursor of the Messiah foretold by the prophet. He is living in the wilderness proclaiming, "Make ready the way of the Lord...." Valleys filled, hills brought low, crooked ways made straight refer to reforming one's life. It means correcting faults and doing penance. The Lord enters into the hearts only of those who are ready to receive him. That means by the rejection of all sinful habits; that means sorrow for our sins.

The best way to prove to God and to ourselves that we are truly sorry is by the practice of prayer, penance and self-denial. Without some penance and self-denial it is impossible to be saved. For, we cannot do and experience everything and still serve God.

It is difficult for us to hear and understand the message of John the Baptist as the proper preparation for Christmas. For, his message of penance and self-denial is diametrically opposed to the culture we live in which is a culture of ease, comfort, pleasure, self-gratification, materialism and consumerism. In our culture self-denial for a religious purpose is considered crazy or fanatic, but at the same time it is considered chic and enlightened if done for reasons of health or beauty or sport, like football or long distance running.

Penance reminds us that we need God's grace. We need his forgiveness, we need his salvation. We depend on him totally. So I urge each one of you to give up something you like in the days before Christmas so you can share the poverty of St. John and Jesus born in a stable – so you can share in that in some small way. It could be a candy bar, a meal, a drink, or turning off TV for an evening and reading a few chapters in the Bible or some pages in a life of your favorite saint.

Conclusion

We should not lose sight of the purpose of Advent and Christmas – to re-live in some small way the coming of God into our world to redeem us, to save us, and to bring us to God. In our own small way we should try to follow the example of John the Baptist and we should try to put his teaching into practice in our own lives. If we do that, then with the prophet Isaiah we can say, "All mankind shall see the salvation of God."

If we prepare for Christmas properly and spiritually, we will experience the true joy of Christ on Christmas day. Then Jesus will be for each one of us truly Emmanuel, that is, God with us. To be united to God, who is infinite goodness and sweetness, is what our hearts desire. That is happiness – and we all desire happiness.

VIGIL OF CHRISTMAS – DECEMBER 24

Readings: Romans 1:1-6; Matthew 1:18-21

God Becomes Man

The Christmas Season is the happiest, most joy-filled time of the year. On Christmas Day we celebrate the birth of our God and Savior in many ways – with trees, lights, decorations, cards, gifts, and festive meals with family and friends.

Why do we do this? We rejoice in this way because we celebrate the birthday of Jesus Christ, our Savior. Actually, we celebrate two births: (1) the birth of God into our world of time and space; and (2) the spiritual birth of all those who believe in Him, are baptized and become members of the Church which is his Mystical Body.

Our faith tells us with certainty that Jesus Christ of Nazareth, born in Bethlehem 2000 years ago, is the natural Son of God and the Second Person of the Blessed Trinity. God became man in Jesus. The whole Trinity did not become man, but only the Word of God, the Wisdom of God, the Second Person. This birth in time means that God assumed our human nature as his own – our flesh in the womb of the Virgin Mary on March 25 (invisible presence), and was born on December 25 (visible presence).

Please note that Mary was not a "single mother." She was already legally married to Joseph even though they had not yet begun to live together. Matthew calls Joseph her "husband." So when the angel Gabriel appeared to her and announced to her that she had been chosen by God to be the mother of the Messiah, and she uttered her consent with her "Fiat," Jesus was conceived within the context of a true marriage.

We know from the Creed that Jesus Christ is God from God, light from light, true God from true God, and consubstantial with the Father.

The birth of Jesus Christ in a humble stable in Bethlehem is the greatest event to take place in the whole history of the world. It is so important that we number the days, weeks and months of the year from the birthday of that Child. No other historical event has or ever will surpass it.

This is such a momentous event that we must ask: Why did God become man? The simple answer is to save us from sin and to offer us eternal life with God. He saved us from the Original Sin which we have inherited from Adam and Eve. This means that we come into this world without the grace of God, which we need in order to go to Heaven. We also come into the world with what the Church calls "concupiscence" which is a tendency or inclination to sin and to rebel against the law of God as given to us in the Ten Commandments.

Jesus also saved us from our own personal sins – mortal and venial sins in imitation of Adam and Eve. They are all various forms of disobedience and rebellion against God. The consequences of sin are horrible. They cause separation from God who is the only source of life and love and goodness. So sin is the greatest evil in the world.

By his life, death and resurrection Jesus has reconciled us with God. Through faith in him and Baptism we become sharers in his divine life of grace; we become children of God, partakers of the divine nature and thus pleasing to God and heirs of Heaven.

Who is this Jesus whose birth we celebrate at Christmas? As I said above, he is the Word of God incarnate; he is the Second Person of the Trinity – the infinite God who created the heavens and the earth and each one of us. He is therefore a divine Person with a human nature. What we mean and experience as a human person does not exist in Jesus; he is a divine Person, not a human person. This of course is a great mystery. Since he is one of us, he is Emmanuel, which means "God with us," as we sing at Christmas.

The incarnation of God in Jesus is God's greatest work in the world of creation for three reasons: (1) because it has

God himself as its purpose or end – to assume flesh from the Virgin Mary and so become man; (2) because it is the supreme manifestation of God's love for man; (3) because of the immense good it brings to all mankind – the possibility of salvation and eternal life.

Conclusion

Because of Jesus Christ of Nazareth we now have hope of eternal life and the means to attain it by his sacraments and his grace. Therefore, we rejoice and celebrate during the Christmas Season.

So may the peace and joy of Christ our Savior be with you today and forever. With the holy angels let us sing in our hearts today: "Glory to God in the highest, and on earth peace to men of good will."

CHRISTMAS: SECOND MASS AT DAWN

Readings: Titus 3:4-7; Luke 2:15-20

God Proves His Love

The Second Mass of Christmas centers on the Humanity of Jesus, the Savior, while the Third Mass emphasizes his divinity. What was previously invisible – God's love for man – now is made visible in the form of a newborn baby. St. Paul says today that "The goodness and kindness of God appears. The Eternal Word who now appears in history was generated by the Father for all eternity; he was born of a virgin mother in Bethlehem in time 2000 years ago; daily he is born in us by the gift of his divine grace in our souls.

The dominant theme of Christmas is love and mercy – the love and mercy of God for man. God's love for us was so great that he became a helpless baby at Bethlehem, born of the Virgin Mary and protected by St. Joseph, his foster father. Why did God do this? He did it to save us from sin and death and to offer us eternal life and happiness by believing in him and living a just and moral life. As a result, Christmas gives rise to feelings of hope for eternal life and joy. St. John says in 3:16, "God so loved the world that he gave his only Son that those who believe in him might not perish but might have everlasting life."

To forgive sins and to give eternal life is something that only God can do since it means taking part in his divine nature. That is what Jesus came to do. By his grace he shares his life with us so that, because of him, we can call him Father, "Our Father." But he is God's natural Son, while we are his adopted children.

In addition to being God, Jesus is also a human being of flesh and blood just like us – born of a human mother. He is God almighty, Creator of the heavens and the earth. He is both human and divine – he has a human nature, but he is not a human person – he is a divine Person, the Second Person of the Blessed Trinity. This is a great mystery which can be grasped only by faith.

Jesus is light and truth – the truth about God, man and the world. He said in John 14:6, "I am the way, the truth and the life." Jesus is our great God and Savior, as St. Paul says in his Letter to Titus (2:13) which is read at the midnight Mass.

Christmas is the happiest time of the year for several reasons: (1) because it is a season permeated with love. At this time we experience God's love for us. It is visible. And in imitation of God's love for us we are motivated to show love for our family and friends; (2) because the greatest happiness in life comes from loving others and being loved. Why is this? Because God made us out of love and for love. That is our destiny. He made us for himself and we know from 1 John 4 that God is love – that is his very nature and definition – and we experience a touch of that love at Christmas.

When we show love for God and love for our neighbor, then we are doing what God made us for, what God made us to do. And when we do that, we experience true joy and happiness. That is why Christmas is such a happy time – a time to rejoice! So saying "Merry Christmas" really means "rejoice" because Jesus has come to save us.

Conclusion

As believers in Christ we have hope of everlasting happiness if we remain faithful to him and his commandments. Through our Baptism he has cleansed us from sin and made us children of God and heirs of Heaven. St. Paul expresses that idea by saying that we become "new creatures." When we look at the manger and consider who Jesus is – both God and Man – surrounded by Mary and Joseph, the shepherds and the animals, we should rejoice and thank God for this great gift – and adore him, just as Mary and Joseph and the shepherds did.

God bless you – and may you enjoy a blessed and holy Christmas with your family and friends. God wants you to rejoice at his coming into the world, for he is Emmanuel – God with us.

SUNDAY WITHIN THE OCTAVE OF CHRISTMAS

Readings: Galatians 4:1-7; Luke 2:33-40

A Sign of Contradiction

When we look at the manger in the dark cave at Bethlehem we see a little newborn child, weak, dependent on his mother, and watched over by St. Joseph and a few animals. But this is no ordinary human child. This is God Almighty in his human nature taken from the holy Virgin. We should note here the difference between what is visible and what is invisible.

There is a great contrast between the visible weakness of the Child and his invisible power; between his present humility and his eternal glory; between his humble obedience to Mary and Joseph and his dignity as the King of the universe.

In the first reading from Galatians St. Paul stresses the humanity of Jesus when he says: "God sent his Son, born of a woman, born under the law...." There may even be just a hint here that Mary is a virgin mother. God became man in Jesus that we might become sons and daughters of God and heirs to his kingdom; that we might participate in his divine nature. Because of his birth he is now our brother and one of us.

In the Incarnation God achieves our redemption through weakness, humility, and suffering in order to atone for sin. This is very hard for us to understand and accept. Old Simeon recognizes him as a suffering Messiah along the lines of Isaiah 53: "He is destined for the fall, the rising of many in Israel – destined to be a sign that is contradicted." Yes, he was contradicted and put to death by his enemies. Salvation and damnation depend on the acceptance or rejection of him, but we still remain free – he will not force himself on us.

Simeon also says that Mary will suffer with Jesus, "a sword will pierce your own soul too." That sword is the sorrow and anguish of the heart of Mary at the sight of the sufferings of her son. Simeon is a prophet inspired by God, as is also the elderly Anna. Both are led by the Holy Spirit to proclaim the Messiah. Simeon and Anna both gave witness to him – that is what we should do in our lives by word and deed – by our lives as faithful Christians in a hostile world.

Jesus, Mary and Joseph fulfilled all the commands of the Jewish Law. They were pious, holy, law-abiding poor people. As a holy family, they are a model for all families. After their stay in Bethlehem they returned to Nazareth, about 80 miles north of Jerusalem, to lead a simple family life in obscurity. St. Luke tells us that the Child grew physically and mentally and became strong. There he led an ordinary life for about thirty years. Some of the characteristics of that life were poverty, obedience, work and prayer. St. Luke also says that "the grace of God was upon him" and he was "full of wisdom and truth."

Jesus grew mentally in the sense that he experienced the details of daily human life. For the most part, his divinity was hidden. A little of it shines through when, as a boy of twelve, he remained in the temple without telling his parents. When Mary questioned him about this he answered, "Did you not know that I must be about my Father's business?" He also let some of his glory shine through his humanity later during the Transfiguration on Mt. Tabor before Peter, James and John.

Conclusion

Jesus Christ, who is the wisdom of God and the Second Person of the Blessed Trinity, is our Savior and our model. If we follow him, if we walk in his ways and keep his commandments, we will lead full, happy lives in this world and will be working out our eternal salvation. We should remember: "He is destined for the fall and resurrection of many" – the fall for those who reject him, and the resurrection for those who follow him. No one can remain indifferent to Christ – each person must either accept or reject him.

We should imitate our Blessed Mother Mary who meditated on these things and pondered them in her heart (see Luke 2:19, 51). Mary is the first Christian and a perfect Christian in humility, faith, obedience to the Father, and constant prayer. As someone has said, she is the woman wrapped in silence. After her comes St. Joseph, the foster father of Jesus, who was the second Christian believer and is now the heavenly patron of the universal Church. We should model our faith, our thinking and our life on Jesus, Mary and Joseph. They show us the way to God and to true and lasting happiness.

JANUARY 1: OCTAVE DAY OF CHRISTMAS

Readings: Titus 2:11-15; Luke 2:21

Time and Eternity

New Year's Day makes us think of time and eternity – Old Man Time signifies the past and the Baby signifies the future New Year. St. Paul tells us in today's Epistle from his Letter to Titus that "The grace of God our Savior has appeared to all men." He is also "our blessed hope" and "our great God and Savior." He sacrificed himself for us that he might redeem us from all iniquity and make us a people acceptable to God, pursuing good works.

In the past the octave day of Christmas, January 1, was called "The Circumcision of Our Lord" and that is indicated by today's short Gospel reading from St. Luke. For, on the eighth day after the birth of Jesus, according to the requirement of the Law of Moses (Leviticus 12:3), he was circumcised, probably by St. Joseph, his foster father. On this day therefore he shed his first drops of blood for us, offering himself completely to the Father as he did on the cross on Calvary thirty-three years later. Because of this first shedding of blood, the circumcision is a type of Calvary.

St. Joseph gave the name of "Jesus" to this special Child as he had been instructed by the angel. The name means "savior" or "the Lord saves." That name is so powerful that anyone who utters it with faith, and does the will of God, will be saved. Even though he was not bound by the Law, Jesus submitted himself to his Father's will in humble obedience. Thus, in this mystery he teaches us to embrace God's will, whatever it might be, in our own lives.

We do not know what awaits us in the New Year, but God knows, since he knows all things. But we should be ready to accept his will with courage and readiness. We should be certain that in his holy will we shall find our peace and sanctification. In all the events of the New Year our prayer should be "Thy will be done," as we pray in the "Our Father."

The coming of the New Year makes us think about the meaning of time and eternity. Time is a measure of motion and is a gift from God. A limited amount of time is given to each person – we are born, we mature, we grow old and we die. The Bible says that the length of a man's life is 70 years – and 80 for those who are strong. Time is precious. It passes and is gone. Time wasted or ill-spent is lost forever; time well-spent is meritorious and has an eternal reward.

Eternity means the possession of complete life all at once with no before or after. In eternity, with the angels and saints in Heaven, we will be fixed forever in the degree of love which we have reached now in time. So now is the time to work out our salvation. Now is the time to grow in the love of God and love of neighbor. Each passing year is a warning to treasure every moment and to sanctify it with charity. Not one of us here present knows for certain that he will be alive on this day a year from now. Fellow parishioners who sat here a year ago have left us and gone into eternity. By acting always out of love, we make each passing moment eternal, permanent, by giving it value in love.

We can sanctify each moment by doing good works with love and generosity. This means doing God's will all the time, every day. Therefore, we should avoid harmful and useless activities that waste time, such as excessive TV watching, reading trashy books and magazines. Time dedicated to God and neighbor, and doing his will, will endure and have an eternal reward. We know that ideas have consequences. Likewise, good works have consequences – eternal consequences. St. Paul says, "Now is the acceptable time… now is the day of salvation" (2 Corinthians 6:2). The wise author of Ecclesiastes tells us: "For everything there is a season, and a time for every matter under Heaven: a time to be born, and a time to die" and so forth (3:1-8). When you get home, I suggest you take out your Bible and read that passage.

Conclusion

On this New Year's Day thank God for the time he has given you so far, and make a firm resolution to use your time in the coming year in a positive way by doing God's will. Give eternal value to each passing moment by using it in performing acts of love of God and neighbor. For, if you live according to God's will, you will find true happiness in this life and you will merit permanent happiness with God forever in the life to come. May our Lord bless you all throughout this New Year.

HOLY NAME OF JESUS

[Sunday between January 1 & 6; otherwise on Jan. 2]

Readings: Acts 4:8-12; Luke 2:21

A Name Above Every Other Name

At the beautiful Shrine of the North American Martyrs in Auriesville, N.Y., the visitor will see the holy name of Jesus in bright red letters nailed to each of the many trees surrounding the Shrine. This is to remind the pilgrim that the last word on the lips of the young martyr, René Goupil, was "Jesus." After being dealt a mortal blow from a tomahawk by an Iroquois Indian, Goupil uttered the holy name of Jesus before he lost consciousness.

The name "Jesus" means "God saves" or simply "Savior." As often in the Old Testament, a person's name indicates his role in salvation history. The Epistle today from the Book of Acts recalls the miraculous act of St. Peter who had cured a cripple at the entrance to the Temple in Jerusalem by invoking the name of Jesus on him: "In the name of Jesus Christ of Nazareth, walk" (Acts 3:6). The man was cured instantly and began to walk and jump for joy. In his defense Peter said to the Jewish leaders who were questioning him about this: "There is salvation in no one else, for there is no other name under Heaven given to men by which we must be saved" (Acts 4:12).

The name given to Jesus came from Heaven. It was given by the Archangel Gabriel to Mary. Joseph was told in a dream to name Mary's child "Jesus." He did that at his circumcision eight days after his birth as we read in today's very short Gospel. The Child is the Son of the Most High, Son of God. He is the Savior of the world. This is no ordinary Child – it is God himself in the flesh who became man to save us.

We see from just one event in the life of Peter that there is great power for good in the name of Jesus. Accordingly, the holy name of Jesus is invoked in all the sacraments and official prayers of the Church. We pray constantly "through Jesus Christ our Lord." The power is not just in the letters and sound of the word. The name stands for the person and in this case it is the Second Person of the Blessed Trinity.

St. John in his Gospel quotes Jesus as saying, "If you ask anything of the Father in my name, he will give it to you; ask and you will receive" (16:23-24). The name of Jesus is all-powerful because it designates the mystery, the power, and the mission of the Son of God who became man to save us from sin and the consequences of sin. To call upon his holy name with truth is to appeal to the infinite merits of his passion, death and resurrection. And this call is always heard by the Father because it is supported by the infinite merits of Jesus the Savior.

The name of Jesus should be treated with reverence and respect because he is the center of history, the joy of every heart, and the answer to all the desires of the human heart. That name is protected by the Second Commandment which tells us not to take God's name in vain. Common sins against the Second Commandment are blasphemy and cursing. Some Christians have the bad habit of uttering the holy name of

Jesus often in daily conversation in order to shock others and to give a certain emphasis to their vain words.

Mankind finds in the holy name of Jesus all that it needs and longs for: peace, pardon, love, freedom, joy and eternal life. St. Bernard loved to sing the glories of the name of Jesus. He said once about that name, I think in a sermon: "It is light when preached, food in meditation, healing when it is invoked.... The name of Jesus is honey in the mouth, music to the ear, gladness in the heart. It is also a remedy for sin and sadness of heart." Whoever calls on this name with faith, will be filled with grace, which is the life of God, and so become a child of God and heir of Heaven. There is no other name like it because it is "life-giving" in the spiritual sense. The Church prays in the Introit for today's Mass, "O Lord, our God, how glorious is your name over all the earth" (quoting Psalm 8:2).

Conclusion

We should pray today as we pray at Benediction of the Blessed Sacrament: "Blessed be the name of Jesus." During the day we should invoke the name of Jesus by saying, "Jesus, Mary and Joseph," or "Most Sacred Heart of Jesus I implore that I may ever love thee more and more" or the famous Jesus prayer: "Lord Jesus Christ, Son of the living God, have mercy on me a sinner." The Divine Mercy prayer given to Sister Kowalska is also appropriate: "Jesus, I trust in you."

I will conclude by citing the opening words in today's Introit, taken from St. Paul's Letter to the Philippians (2:10-11): "In the name of Jesus let every knee bow, of those that are in Heaven, on earth, and under the earth: and let every tongue confess that the Lord Jesus Christ is in the glory of God the Father." Today on the feast of the Holy Name of Jesus those words should be in our heart and on our lips.

EPIPHANY

Readings: Isaiah 60:1-6; Matthew 2:1-12

Light of the World

The feast of the Epiphany is about light and darkness, grace and sin. It is an essential part of the Christmas Season. The word here means the "appearance" or "self-manifestation" of God to the world in the sense that God reveals himself to the Gentiles. The emphasis on light and the star signify the revelation of divine truth about God and man's destiny – why he is here on this earth.

The point is that Jesus is the King of the Jews, a descendant in the royal line of David, the Messiah or Anointed One and the fulfillment of the prophecies of the Old Testament because he is both God and man. It is not the oracle in Isaiah 60 that gives rise to the story (as many say today), but it is the event that illustrates the words and events of the Old Testament. We should remember that Matthew wrote his Gospel about ten to twenty years after Jesus' death so he knows that Jesus Christ is God in the flesh.

The three wise men from the east – from Arabia or Persia – have been given the names of Gaspar, Balthasar and Melchior. Matthew does not call them "kings," but the gifts they give suggest that they might have been nobles of some kind.

Having been led on by the mysterious star, they arrived in Jerusalem and asked the officials there "where the newborn King of the Jews" might be found. In ancient thinking, heavenly signs accompanied the birth of an important person. This was reported, for example, as having happened at the birth of Alexander the Great and Julius Caesar. King Herod was "troubled" because he was worried about a rival to his kingship. Matthew adds that "all Jerusalem with him" was also troubled, that is, the Jewish leaders. Perhaps they were upset because they did not know what Herod, a bloody and ruthless ruler, might do. Herod asked the chief priests and the scribes of the people where the Christ should be born. They say in Bethlehem of Judea, referring to a prophecy of Micah 5:1-3. That was the birthplace of King David and the Messiah was to come from his line.

Herod pretends to the Magi that he wants to go and pay homage to the new King. Here we see his cunning and deceit and the Magi probably suspected the same thing. We know he was not sincere from subsequent events in the bloody slaughter of the Holy Innocents.

A star, or a bright heavenly light like a star, led them to the cave where Jesus was born. It was probably a miraculous light and because of this light we now decorate our homes and trees with lights as a sign of the truth of Jesus Christ. When the Magi saw the star "they rejoiced exceedingly." Joy is mentioned often in St. Luke's Gospel but only sparingly in Matthew. Here we see that God's revelation, his light, when humbly received, causes great joy in the human heart.

Next Matthew says that they worshipped him or gave him homage as a very special person. Each of the three gifts presented has a definite signification. Gold was a sign of kings so it means that the Child is a King. Incense was used for worship of God so it indicates that he is a Priest. Myrrh was a spice used in burials; this is an omen of his death since he will die like the prophets. Finally, they were warned in a dream not to return to Herod and so they left immediately for their own country. Here is an indication that God directs history. From the whole story we see the different responses to the birth of the Child on the part of the Jewish leaders and the Gentiles – the Jews rejected Jesus but the Gentiles accepted him and believed in him.

We learn in today's Epistle that the Epiphany illustrates the prophecies of the Old Testament. Matthew selects texts from the Old Testament that portray Jesus as the King of the Jews. "Be enlightened, O Jerusalem: for thy light is come, and the glory of the Lord is risen upon thee." "The Gentiles shall walk in thy light, and kings in the brightness of thy rising." This means that Christ is the light of the nations, the "*lumen gentium*," the opening words of Vatican II's document on the Church. "All they from Saba shall come, bringing gold and frankincense and showing forth praise to the Lord." The Gentiles coming to Jerusalem means that all are called to join the Church.

We should remember that the Gospels recount historical events, but the primary interest is theological. So the story of the Epiphany is telling us that there were wise men from the east who came to Bethlehem to pay homage to the baby Jesus. They represent all peoples and nations. We can detect three characteristics of the Magi: (1) they were searchers – they followed the star looking for the truth; (2) they were discoverers because they found what they were looking for in spite of all difficulties; (3) they persevered until they found what they were looking for – the King of the Jews.

The wise men responded to the graces given them and followed the mysterious light. Let us follow the light given to us which means that we should be faithful to the graces given to us – we should follow our own star.

Conclusion

That star or light will lead us to the adoration of the child Jesus. Like the Magi, we should offer precious gifts – not gold, frankincense and myrrh, which are consumed and pass away like all temporal things – but more excellent, spiritual and lasting gifts of love, obedience, humility and keeping the Commandments. Accordingly, we can offer ourselves to him at this Mass. Finally, today let us make our own the Communion Antiphon of the Mass: "We have seen his star in the east, and have come, with gifts, to adore the Lord." God bless you.

HOLY FAMILY

Readings: Colossians 3:12-17; Luke 2:42-52

God First

Today we commemorate the most perfect human family that ever existed: Jesus, Mary and Joseph, the Holy Family in Nazareth. The family is the basis of every human society and is defined as a group of persons living together who are related by blood or marriage. Not just any group of persons who agree to live together is a family.

This family is called "holy" because of its closeness to God who is holiness itself and Jesus is the Son of God, the Word who lived in the family of the Father and the Holy Spirit for all eternity.

The Holy Family is the model for all families because they put God first in everything – and God was always present, not only physically, but also in their thoughts. Outwardly it seemed to be a normal poor family, but in reality it was unique, since Jesus is the Son of God and Mary is his Virgin Mother.

The Church teaches us that marriage and the family are of divine institution (see Genesis 1 & 2); it is not the result of blind evolution. In his public life, at the wedding feast of Cana, Jesus elevated the natural contract of marriage to the level of a sacrament which confers sanctifying grace, the life of the soul. The purpose of marriage, described by Vatican II as "a communion of life and love," is the generation and education of children and the well-being of the spouses.

Families are the basic building blocks of civil society and also of Church life. Vocations to the priesthood and the religious life come mainly from healthy families, especially from large families. Today many families are dysfunctional because of contraception, divorce, abortion, infidelity, drugs and alcohol, television and Internet pornography. This is one reason for the serious decline in vocations to the priesthood and religious life.

Recent documents of the Church refer to the family as a "domestic church" – and it has also been called "the Mystical Body of Christ in miniature."

Vatican Council II says that the Catholic family should be characterized by the mutual affection of its members, and by the common prayer they offer to God (Laity #11). "Mutual affection" here means love and respect for each other, and obedience to God and to one's parents, as spelled out by St. Paul in today's Epistle. "Common prayer" in the family is necessary for harmonious living together. Fr. Patrick Peyton, the Rosary priest, was right on target when he said over and over again: "The family that prays together stays together." Both of these, mutual affection and common prayer, are found in a perfect way in the Holy Family of Nazareth.

St. Luke tells us today in the Gospel Reading: "When Jesus was twelve years old, they went up to Jerusalem according to the custom of the feast." They observed all the requirements of the Law of Moses. We also have obligations to God. Do we observe them as the Holy Family did – Sunday Mass, daily prayers, keeping the Commandments, loving one another?

Then something unusual happens in Jerusalem: Jesus separated himself from his parents for a time; he remained in Jerusalem when they departed for home. Thus he caused them great anxiety and grief. Sometimes he does the same to us. He seems to abandon us, but he is really not absent, only hidden. At times God tests our love for him – we see this often in the lives of the saints. If we do not give up, but seek him constantly, we will find him, just as Mary and Joseph found the Child Jesus in the Temple. That is where we will find him too – in church and in prayer.

This is a great mystery. Jesus, the Word of God, was taught by the Scribes and Pharisees. What humility! Infinite wisdom subjects himself to human wisdom. He asked questions and gave answers to their questions and all were amazed at his wisdom. We can always learn more about our Catholic faith because it is an inexhaustible treasure of truth about God and man. Much of that truth is contained in the *Catechism of the Catholic Church* and a copy of it should be in every Catholic home.

St. Luke informs us that, after the Jerusalem trip, Jesus went down to Nazareth and was subject to Mary and Joseph. There he advanced in wisdom, stature and grace. This period is called his "hidden life" in which we see certain characteristics.

Growth. In the following years Jesus grew physically, psychologically and intellectually. What he knew by his divine intellect he now learned in a new way by the growth of his human consciousness, by living and working in a human family. This is part of the mystery of the Incarnation. But note that he spent thirty years in his hidden life and only three years in his public life of preaching the Gospel.

Poverty. The Holy Family was poor but not destitute. They had the necessities of life, a home and food, and they were able to travel to Jerusalem, which probably took ten days to two weeks.

Work. Jesus worked for a living as a carpenter. He shared in the toil, sweat and exhaustion of physical labor.

Obedience. Jesus was obedient to Mary and Joseph, individual persons whom he had created. Because of that his home in Nazareth has been called "the house of obedience." In this Jesus gives us an example of obedience to all legitimate authority.

Mary, his Mother, is a mystic, a contemplative in action. St. Luke tells us that she kept all these things in her heart and pondered on them. During those years in Nazareth, what did they talk about at table? How much of his divine wisdom did Jesus reveal to Mary and Joseph? We do not know. But they must have discussed the history of Israel, the Law of Moses, and the prophets. Jesus would have helped them to understand God's plan of creation and redemption. Here we see the author of Scripture explaining it to his parents, as he did after his resurrection to the two disciples on the road to Emmaus.

Conclusion

The Church urges us today to love the Holy Family and to try to imitate Jesus, Mary and Joseph in our own family life. The key to that imitation is to put God first in our life. This leads to mutual affection which is nourished and increased by common prayer. St. Paul tells us how to do it in the Epistle: "Put on, as God's chosen ones, holy and beloved, a heart of mercy, kindness, humility, meekness, patience. Bear with one another and forgive one another."

SECOND SUNDAY AFTER EPIPHANY

Readings: Romans 12:6-16; John 2:1-11

Mary's Power of Intercession with Jesus

A wedding is a happy event when a man and a woman are joined together for life in a fruitful union. To show our joy we celebrate the marriage with a party and banquet with music and an abundance of food and drink. In today's Gospel Reading we have the beautiful account of Jesus and Mary at the wedding feast at Cana in Galilee. Cana is a small village not far from Nazareth. The Holy Family was probably related to the bride or the groom.

By his presence and the record of it in the Gospel of John Jesus blessed marriage and elevated it to the level of a Sacrament, that is, he changed it from a natural contract to an efficacious sign of divine grace. The prophets Hosea and Isaiah compare God's love for Israel to the love of a bridegroom for his bride. So marriage is a symbol of Jesus' love for his Church which is the New Israel. He is the Bridegroom and she is the bride.

There are two levels of meaning in the account of the wedding feast at Cana. On the literal level, it means that Jesus, Mary and his disciples were invited to the wedding. Mary notices a shortage of wine, which will embarrass the families of the bride and groom. Perhaps it was caused by the presence of Jesus' thirsty disciples. Mary says to Jesus that they have no wine. Jesus' answer to her is difficult to interpret: "Woman, what is that to thee and to me?" It seems to mean something like: "Why are you saying this to me?" In any event, Mary tells the servants to "Do whatever he tells you." Mary is certain that he will do something to solve the embarrassing situation. Jesus seems to object, but he does her bidding. It should be noted that these are the last words of Mary recorded in the Gospels. They were recorded for our benefit that we too should do what he tells us, namely, to believe in him and to follow him.

The six stone jars held about 150 gallons of water. By a mere act of his will Jesus changes the water into excellent wine. The servants take some to the head waiter who then complains to the groom that this good wine should have been served first. This was Jesus' first miracle. St. John calls it his first "sign," that is, the first sign of his divinity. John says that "he manifested his glory, and his disciples believed in him" – believed that he is the Messiah. His divinity, his divine power shone through his humanity.

There is also a spiritual meaning to this miracle event. We note that Mary is observant, caring and that she intercedes with her Son for the couple without being asked. Thus, she is our powerful intercessor with her Son on our behalf. We give expression to this when we recite the "Hail Mary" and say "Pray for us sinners now and at the hour of our death."

Jesus uses his divine power for the first time because his Mother asked him to do something for the embarrassed couple. Note also the abundance of high quality wine – about 150 gallons. An abundance of wine is a sign of the age of the Messiah according to Genesis 49:11-12. It is also a sign of redemption and Heaven.

The wedding feast at Cana prompts us to reflect on the nature of Christian marriage. It shows us that Matrimony is willed by God and is a sacrament. He created man male and female so that they complement each other. Marriage is characterized by its unity – meaning one man and one woman. It is also indissoluble for life. Accordingly, marriage is an image of Jesus' eternal love for his bride, the Church.

The Church teaches us that marriage has two purposes or ends. The two are the procreation and education of children and the unity of the spouses – the intimate love between husband and wife. Vatican II said that marriage is a communion of life and love or a partnership of life and love.

Because of its unity and indissolubility marriage requires proper preparation as one would prepare for any profession. Marriage requires maturity: an adult understanding of the nature of marriage, a sense of responsibility, and a loving commitment – which means the readiness to sacrifice oneself for one's spouse. Marriage is the normal means for Catholics to work out their eternal salvation. It also has eternal consequences for the spouses and their children.

Some of the obstacles of a successful marriage are selfishness, materialism, contraception, abortion, and a lack of respect for women.

Conclusion

At Cana Jesus manifested his power over nature. Without using words, by an act of his will, he changed water into wine. As the poet said, "God looked at the water, and the water blushed." There is also a hint here of the Eucharist. For, if Jesus has the power to change water into wine, he can also turn bread into his Body and wine into his Blood.

There is a hint too of what Jesus can do to us if we trust in him. Jesus' power to change water into wine is a sign of what his grace can do to change us into children of God and heirs of Heaven.

St. John tells us that his disciples "believed in him." We are his disciples and we believe in him. He loves us as a bridegroom loves his bride. During this Mass each one should ask Jesus to increase his faith by praying: "O Jesus, I beg you to transform my soul as you once transformed water into wine for the bride and groom at Cana."

THIRD SUNDAY AFTER EPIPHANY

Readings: Romans 12:16-21; Matthew 8:1-13

Overcome Evil with Good

St. Paul's Epistle today echoes Jesus' Sermon on the Mount when he said: "You have heard it said of old, 'An eye for an eye and a tooth for a tooth,' but I say to you, 'Love your enemies; do good to those who hate you.'" This is a hard saying from Jesus, because it is difficult to love one's enemies – to love those who hate you, that is, to wish them good and not evil. However, this is the Christian way, and if we are serious followers of Christ we must imitate him. Consider how, while hanging in agony on the cross, Jesus forgave his enemies: "Father, forgive them for they know not what they do." It is not sufficient to say, "Well, Jesus was God so he could do it, but I cannot." He is telling us all to forgive our enemies and he also gives us the grace to do it, if we only ask for it.

It is not up to us to punish sinners; God is the one who will punish them. "Vengeance is mine, I will repay, says the Lord" (Deuteronomy 32:35). God is better able to judge others and punish them than we are because he knows all things and all circumstances of every sin and event. We cannot read the hearts of others, but he can. People often ask why others do what they do, but usually we do not know the motives of others, unless they tell us.

St. Paul urges us, "Be not overcome by evil, but overcome evil by good." This means that Catholics should avoid the sin of revenge, which means inflicting harm or injury on another in return for an injury received. For, when we are injured, we often get angry and want to get even. Revenge causes the evil of another person to lead us into the same sin. Two wrongs do not make a right. The avenger suffers physically and spiritually because nursing resentment harms both mind and body.

We all need forgiveness from God, but God does not forgive those who do not forgive others. Forgiveness means the pardon of an offense. Every time we pray the "Our Father" we say: "Father, forgive us our trespasses as we forgive those who trespass against us." That is a very important "as."

In recent years even atheists and agnostics have discovered the value and beneficial results of forgiveness. And we should remember that our prayers and sacrifices to God are not acceptable to him if we are not reconciled with others. St. Paul tells us today, "If it be possible, as much as is in you, have peace with all men." When we are at peace with others, we are at peace within ourselves.

"Overcome evil by good." Jesus tells us to be meek and humble as he was. Kindness and gentleness in dealing with others, no matter who they are but first of all in our own family, often work wonders in human relations. We see an example of that in the two miracle stories in today's Gospel Reading – Jesus cured the ill with a touch and a word. Revenge, however – returning evil for evil – tends to perpetuate itself. We see an example of this in the constant wars in the Middle East.

St. Paul tells us (quoting Proverbs 25:21), "If thy enemy be hungry, give him to eat: if he thirsts, give him to drink: for doing this, thou shalt heap coals of fire upon his head."

That is, he will suffer burning shame at seeing you return good for evil. And the fire of remorse may lead him to contrition and reconciliation.

Good example often converts others. Look at the good example of the saints: St. Francis of Assisi, St. Maximilian Kolbe, St. Pio. Then there is the example of John Paul II. Who can forget the picture of him visiting his assassin in prison and offering him his forgiveness? Also remember the forgiveness of the father in the parable of the Prodigal Son. He waited for his son to return – and ran to meet him.

Conclusion

Finally, our Blessed Lord gave us an example of returning good for evil when he forgave those who put him to death on Calvary. St. Peter expresses this well in his First Epistle: "When he was reviled, he did not revile in return; when he suffered he did not threaten; but he delivered himself to him (i.e., Pilate) that judged him unjustly" (1 Peter 2:23).

Again, in the "Our Father" we pray: "Father, forgive us our trespasses AS we forgive those who trespass against us." May God grant us all the grace to forgive those who have offended us. The more we forgive, the more we will be forgiven. Note these words of Jesus in Matthew 7:2, "The measure you give will be the measure you get." So, the more forgiving we are, the more God will forgive us – and we all need forgiveness. God bless you.

FOURTH SUNDAY AFTER EPIPHANY

Readings: Romans 13:8-10; Matthew 8:23-27

We Are All in the Same Boat

Today's Mass is the 4th Sunday after Epiphany, filling in for an extra Sunday after Pentecost. The main point in today's

Gospel Reading about the disciples' fear of drowning is that we should have more trust in God and his providence.

When they wake Jesus up he says to them, "Why are you fearful, O you of little faith?" (Matthew 8:26). Some of the writers in the early Church said in reference to this passage that God caused the storm in the lake purposely as a test of the Apostles' trust in him. They regarded the storm as a symbol of the trials and troubles that make the life of each one of us somewhat storm-tossed – some more, some less. In a certain sense, we can say that we are all in the same boat. So it would be good for us to learn the lessons to be drawn from the conduct of the Apostles and also of Jesus.

The Apostles did show some confidence in God because they asked Jesus for his help. He was sleeping but still present in their midst. Sometimes we get the feeling that God is sleeping and not paying any attention to us and our prayers. But the Apostles' appeal implied that they had faith in his power to save them.

It is clear from Jesus' words that the Apostles were weak in their trust in Jesus – "of little faith," he said. Apparently they relied on their own efforts and appealed to him only as a last resort. They wake Christ up – as if he did not know their plight and as if he could not help them even as he slept. They also awaken him in panic because they are frightened to death. They are near despair, saying, "Lord, save us, we are perishing!" With the author of life in the same boat with them, they fear death by drowning. So they do not yet have complete trust in him – and he is testing them. St. Mark, in his account of the miracle, adds here, "Master, is it no concern to you that we perish?" (4:38) Then Jesus asks them, "Why are you fearful, O you of little faith?" Jesus indicates here that faith should drive out fear which is anxiety about impending evil. Faith includes not only belief in God, but also trust and confidence in him and his providence. So Jesus puts his finger on the real cause of fear – not the storm, trials or temptations but lack of trust in him. We all need trust in God which is reliance on the help of another; it contains an aspect also of hope when placed in God, having confidence that he will give us the grace we need to remain faithful to Him.

The above conversation took place while Jesus was reclining, and the storm raged about them. We see here that Jesus was more concerned about their interior life of faith than he was about the storm and the waves. Then "He arose and rebuked the wind and the sea, and there came a great calm." Matthew is telling us here that Jesus not only drives out devils, cures the sick, raises the dead, and so forth. He also commands the forces of nature and they obey him. The Apostles naturally were amazed at seeing this. Who wouldn't be? Especially anyone who has been in a real stormy sea. And they said, "What manner of man is this, that even the wind and the sea obey him?" There is an allusion here to Genesis 1 and the creative power of God who created the heavens and the earth and established order among the forces of nature.

Conclusion

We should expect storms and trials in this life as a testing of our faith. God does not tempt us, but he allows us to be tempted by the world, the flesh and the devil. Even when we think God pays no attention to us, we should trust in His concern and power – and persevere in prayer and good works, saying, "Lord, help me!"

Each one should make the act of faith contained in the Collect of today's Mass: "O God, you know that our weakened nature cannot withstand the dangers that surround us. Make us strong in mind and body, so that with your help we may be able to overcome the afflictions that our own sins have brought upon us. We ask this through Christ, Our Lord. Amen."

FIFTH SUNDAY AFTER EPIPHANY

Readings: Colossians 3:12-17; Matthew 13:24-30

The Problem of Evil

Pope Paul VI said that the parable of the wheat and the weeds, in today's Gospel Reading, was for him the most difficult to understand of all the parables. A parable is an instructive story that makes us think divine and saving truth is hidden behind the vivid images. This parable is indeed difficult to understand. And once we come to see the point of it, that point is hard to accept and put into practice, for it deals with the presence of evil in the world and in the Church. It also deals with God's forbearance, his patience with the evil perpetrated by men and women.

It is important here to realize that evil is not a positive reality. Evil is the absence of a good that should be present; for example, a person is born blind or without hands – things a human being should have to be complete. But it is not evil for a rock to lack eyes or hands because a rock is not supposed to have them.

The meaning of the various parts of the parable is not difficult. The sower is the Son of Man or Jesus; the field is the world; the good seed are faithful Christians; the weeds are the followers of the devil; the enemy is the devil; the harvesters are the angels and the harvest is the end of the world. At harvest time, just as the weeds are separated from the wheat and burned, so will it be at the end of the world: evil doers will be cast into hell and the just will "shine like the sun" in the Father's kingdom.

It is hard for us to accept that God allows both to grow to maturity. He is in no hurry to punish evildoers, for he desires that they repent and turn back to him. This parable is definitely not a lesson in farming or agriculture; rather, it is about how God deals with us, his children. We should be happy that he is very patient and forbearing with us, for he knows how weak we are and prone to evil.

As each one of us knows, there are many horrible evils in the world, not only tsunamis, earthquakes and plagues, which are independent of man's will, but there are also personal crimes like murder, theft, adultery, lying, hatred and blasphemy.

God tolerates much evil. It could be in personal suffering, such as the sudden death of a loved one; evil in the world – corruption in politics, war, abortion, euthanasia, unchecked pornography in the media; evil in the Church – heretics, dissenters, weak and sinful bishops and priests.

There will always be evil because of original sin and fallen man. That is why our Lord gave us the Sacrament of Penance. Sometimes we are tempted to cry out: If God is really good and omnipotent, why does he allow this to go on? Why doesn't he stop it? We know that God wants all to turn to his love, but he is not in a hurry as we often are. Usually, God does not punish the sinner immediately. He gives him time and offers his grace to bring him to repentance. As examples of this, we might think of Mary Magdalene, the Good Thief, and Peter who denied him.

In the parable of the weeds we learn that God allows both good and evil to grow together until the harvest time. The evil test the virtue of the good and God is merciful to the evil. Jesus established the Church as a means to bring all to God. The Church is intended for all and embraces both saints and sinners. God is patient, but a time of reckoning will come at the "harvest" when the unrepentant evil will be punished forever and the good will be rewarded in Heaven – forever. That will take place at the Second Coming of Christ and the general judgment.

At times we all wonder why God allows evil to exist. There is no answer to that question that is completely satisfying. St. Augustine wrestled with this problem for many years and finally came to the conclusion that God is so powerful that he can bring good out of evil. Suffering often leads to heroic virtues, for example, in martyrs and sinners dying from cancer who make a deathbed conversion. But evil remains very mysterious to us. It tests our faith to believe that God is good, no matter what he allows to happen. God does not tempt us and does not will moral evil, but he does permit it. We must realize that his ways are not our ways, as Isaiah says in chapter 55.

The best answer I know is love of God and love of neighbor: that is Christianity in a nutshell. We overcome evil by being loving and doing good, by being patient and merciful, by imitating Jesus on the cross. Suffering evil, whether physical or moral, is more bearable when the sufferer thinks of the crucifixion that Jesus endured for the sins of all men. All suffering, offered up in reparation for personal sins and the sins of others, and in union with the Redeemer, can win grace for souls and merit Heaven.

St. Paul gives us the key in the Epistle for today: "Put on a heart of mercy, kindness, humility, meekness and patience. Bear with one another and forgive one another.... But above all these things have charity, which is the bond of perfection.... And may the peace of Christ reign in your hearts.... Show yourselves thankful. Let the word of Christ dwell in you abundantly. Whatever you do in word or in work, do all in the name of the Lord Jesus Christ, giving thanks to God the Father through Jesus Christ Our Lord."

If we strive to live like that, we will be able to deal with and triumph over all the evil and suffering that come our way. Christ did it and he assures us that we also can do it with his grace – if we follow him and imitate him.

SIXTH SUNDAY AFTER EPIPHANY

Readings: 1 Thessalonians 1:2-10; Matthew 13:31-35

The Power of the Gospel

Jesus was a powerful teacher – the greatest teacher of all time. He used concrete stories and vivid examples to get across divine truths of spiritual realities. His teaching is both simple and profound so that his words contain something for the child, the adult and the professor. Today's Gospel offers two such stories or parables for our reflection.

A parable is an instructive story or comparison of one thing with another. Each parable is a mystery; it contains hidden truth and only those can penetrate it who believe in Jesus Christ and listen to his Church.

Today the Church proposes two of Jesus' parables from Matthew's chapter 13. A mustard seed is quite small, but it produces a large plant in Galilee – it can develop into a bush that is 8 to10 feet high. It is large enough to accommodate birds and their nests.

Jesus said to the crowd following him, "The Kingdom of Heaven is like a grain of mustard seed which a man took and sowed in his field." In this parable the man is Jesus; the field is the world; the seed is the word of God or the Gospel. The point is that the beginning is small. The Church began with his Mother Mary, the other holy women, the Apostles and the other disciples – all together about 120 persons in the Upper Room on Easter Sunday. Animated by the Holy Spirit, the mystical body of Christ will spread out in all directions and reach into every part of the world. Through the efforts of the Apostles, St. Paul and their successors Christianity spread throughout the known world of the time.

The growth and power of the word of God applies to each one of us. If we receive the word of God within us and let it grow, it will bring us closer and closer to God. We will grow constantly strong in faith, hope and love.

There is a second short parable in today's Gospel which we should reflect on: the parable of the leaven. The leaven or yeast in the dough is the Gospel; the flour is the world. A small amount of yeast permeates the whole mass of flour. We can also consider the yeast in the parable as divine grace in the life of each individual. The point is that the Gospel of Jesus, working quietly, will permeate and influence the whole world. We should think here of the Christian virtues of love, compassion, mercy, forgiveness and respect for the dignity of each human person. These were brought to their perfection by Jesus and St. Paul praises them in today's Epistle.

Since the time of Christ every part of the world has been touched by Christ through his Gospel and the preaching of his bishops and priests, some more and some less. But the drama of conversion to Christ still goes on – millions are being converted today in Africa and Korea. Many missionaries have testified to the truth of Christ by shedding their blood for him as martyrs. Tertullian put it well in the 3rd century when he said that the blood of martyrs is the seed of Christians.

Think of the influence of Pope John Paul II over a period of 25 years. He spoke to three and a half billion people either in person or by television. Think of what Bishop Sheen did on radio, TV and with his many books. Think of the influence for good of Mother Teresa of Calcutta, St. Francis of Assisi and St. Thomas More.

The word of God and God's grace also work in the life of each one of us like yeast in a batch of dough. We should let it permeate our life and affect our thinking and our choices. As we grow in faith and holiness it should affect everything we say and do. For example, the Gospel helps us to pray daily, to tell the truth always, to act justly towards all, to be charitable and kind towards others, and to follow the Golden Rule: "Do unto others as you would have them do unto you." The negative version of that principle is: "Don't do to others what you don't want them to do to you." God's grace also helps us to overcome temptations and tendencies to evil which we have inherited from Adam because of original sin.

St. Matthew tells us that Jesus always used parables in his teaching. So Matthew sees Jesus as the fulfillment of all the prophecies of the Old Testament. The idea here is that, in some way however obscurely, everything Jesus did was foretold in the Old Testament. St. Augustine put it this way: "The New Testament was hidden in the Old, and the Old Testament is made clear in the New."

To prove his point, Matthew quotes Psalm 78:2, "I will open my mouth in parables. I will utter things hidden since the foundation of the world." Thus, the prophet foretold that the coming Messiah would teach in parables. Jesus did that.

What are these "hidden things"? They are that God planned to become man in Jesus Christ and to save the world by dying on the cross. This is the "mystery" or "plan of God" that St. Paul speaks about in Ephesians and Colossians. Those things, like the Trinity and the Incarnation, are made known to us by the Church and are expressed briefly in the creed which we pray at each Sunday Mass.

Conclusion

It is up to each one of us, as a practicing Catholic, to be part of the leaven or yeast of Christ in society today. Accordingly, we should be witnesses at home, at work, at school, with our friends, and in civic life. We do that by believing in him and by living according to his principle of love of God and neighbor.

SEPTUAGESIMA SUNDAY

Readings: 1 Corinthians 9:27-10:5; Matthew 20:1-26

The Generous Householder

On Septuagesima Sunday, which means seventy days before Easter, there is a change in emphasis in the liturgy from the joy of the coming of the Savior during the Christmas Season to sobering thoughts about what it cost our Lord to atone for sin. There is an emphasis on how much we all need the grace of his atoning death for sin and what we must do in order to share in his divine life.

Today's Gospel reading presents a perplexing parable – at first sight it looks like a case of gross injustice. The workers did not get equal pay for equal work. They received the same pay for unequal work. If an employer did that today he would have trouble with the local union, perhaps a strike and he might be sent to jail for practicing discrimination. But the parable is not a lesson in social justice. Rather, it directs our minds to God – represented by the employer. The vineyard stands for our vocation in life.

If we examine the parable closely we see that no injustice was done to the workmen. Those hired at dawn and later agreed to work for the normal daily wage of the time – a denarius. At the end of the day they each received a day's pay for the work they did – some more some less. The first hired complained about the equal pay to those who came later – 9 a.m., 12, 3 and 5 p.m. The householder said, "I am free to do with my money as I see fit. Are you envious because I am generous?" The employer is both just and generous. His action was not arbitrary; it was motivated by mercy and generosity for those hired later in the day. He shows compassion for them since they get a full day's pay. The reaction of the first-hired workers is natural, but based on purely human reasoning. We must be careful not to imitate them in complaining about God's dealings with us, and we must avoid envy about his generosity to others.

God has been generous to each one of us. He created us and gave us a share in his divine life by grace. He calls us to eternal bliss with him in Heaven. He raised us to the supernatural level and now invites us to strive for holiness.

Jesus was generosity incarnate. He changed 600 quarts of water into good wine at Cana; he caused a miraculous catch of fish on the lake of Galilee; he multiplied a few loaves to feed over 5,000 persons; he cured hundreds of sick people and poured out the last drop of his blood to redeem you and me.

Jesus, the generous God-Man, has told us to be generous in our turn: "Give and it shall be given to you; good measure, pressed down, shaken together, running over shall they pour into your lap. For with what measure you measure... it will be measured to you" (Luke 6:38).

If we look at ourselves objectively, we will see that everything we have, except our sins, is a free gift from God. If others have received more, we have no reason to complain or to be envious. Some have more physical and mental gifts. Some have more grace than others because God does not deal with all alike. Mary, Joseph, the Apostles, Paul, the martyrs and saints were given special graces. But all have sufficient grace to be saved. Those who receive more have more responsibility and will be judged accordingly on the last day.

The Good Thief "stole" Heaven at the last moment – he came at the eleventh hour. Some struggle all their lives to be virtuous and to save their souls. Others, after a life of sin and self-indulgence, make a death-bed conversion and are saved. Think of St. Paul, the persecutor, on the road to Damascus. Who are we to think or say it is not fair? God has been good to me. Should I not rejoice to see him show mercy to the old sinner?

The ways of God with man are unfathomable to us. God is mystery by his very nature. We do not understand him or his thinking or his governance of the world. Isaiah quotes

God as saying: "My thoughts are not your thoughts, nor are your ways my ways. As high as the heavens are above the earth, so high are my ways above your ways" (Isaiah 55:8-9). We cannot grasp or comprehend the goodness and mercy and generosity of God.

I have spoken about God's generosity, mirrored in the example of the employer of the laborers in the vineyard. We are those workers in the vineyard – in our own life growing in virtue and giving good example to others. The vineyard is the service of God; the Master is God; the day is our life; the steward is Jesus the judge; the denarius coin is divine grace, the life of the soul. God's call goes out to all, but some receive more: "Many are called, but few are chosen."

We must remember that God owes us nothing. He says, "Am I not free to do as I please with my money? Or are you envious because I am generous?" We should be careful not to envy the good fortune of others. Our response should be thankfulness for what we have received and joy at the good fortune of others.

Conclusion

God does not deal with us in strict justice – we can thank him for that. If he did, we would all be lost. We should praise and thank God often for his goodness, as the Church does in the Psalms. The Psalms are full of such sentiments, for example in Psalm 145: "The Lord is generous and merciful, slow to anger and of great kindness. The Lord is good to all and compassionate toward all his works" (vv. 8-9). Also, remember the words of God in Isaiah 55:8, "For my thoughts are not your thoughts, nor are your ways my ways, says the Lord."

At the end of the day the householder says to the workers: "Take what is thine and go; I choose to give to this last even as to thee. Have I not a right to do as I choose? Or, are you envious because I am generous?"

SEXAGESIMA SUNDAY

Readings: 2 Corinthians 11:19-33; 12:1-9; Luke 8:4-15

God's Word Is Like a Seed

In the 18th century Ben Franklin received the gift of a broom made in India. While examining it, he found some seeds and decided to plant them. They thrived in American soil and gave birth to American broom straw. Those little seeds contained a hidden power.

Today's Gospel Reading tells us that God's word is like a seed – it has great power that is not visible or immediately evident. It is a living, divine seed of power to change human lives. The Gospel tells us about the divine seed or word and what it can do if it is accepted. In the Epistle for today we see what it accomplished in the life of St. Paul. He preached the Gospel throughout the known world of the time, encountering great personal suffering, but he persevered and had much success.

In the Parable of the Sower, the sower is Jesus, the seed is the word of God, and the different kinds of soil stand for different responses, on the part of those who hear the word, to God's word and his grace.

The parable mentions four types of people who receive the seed of the divine word in different ways. It compares them to the hard ground, to the stony soil, to earth choked with thorns, and to good fertile land.

The seed that falls on hard ground refers to individuals who are worldly, frivolous, wholly taken up with the things of this world. They are immersed in sin and give little or no thought to eternity and what will happen to them when they die.

The seed that falls on stony ground stands for those who are superficial in their devotion and love of God. Their faith is based on emotion primarily rather than on knowledge and conviction. When trouble comes their way, they are easily discouraged and turn to earthly satisfactions.

The seed that falls into ground covered with thorns stands for those who are preoccupied with the pleasures of this world. The seed takes some root, but it is crushed and suffocated by the thorns, namely, the pleasures of this life. An example of this would be students from good Catholic families who go to college and lose their faith.

The seed that falls on good ground refers to those who are truly seeking to find God and to do his will. They receive the word with joy and beg God for the grace to understand it and to put it into practice. The seed flourishes and produces fruit in proportion to the way in which it is received. If the hearer of the word prays, practices some self-denial, attends Mass regularly, strives to love God above all things and his neighbor as himself, that person will produce abundant spiritual fruit. One who ponders the word of God in his heart, as Mary did, in time will grow holy and become more like God.

Two principles are involved here: (1) There must be effort on our part, and (2) cooperation with God's grace which is offered to all, for God desires the salvation of all, as St. Paul says in 1 Timothy 2:4. The kind of fruit Jesus means is supernatural acts of faith, hope and charity, along with observance of all the Commandments. In today's Epistle we see what God's word accomplished in St. Paul one hundred percent. He accepted God's word, lived it, preached it to others, and persevered in the faith to the end when he shed his blood for Christ by being beheaded by the Romans.

Conclusion

The Parable of the Sower is directed to each one of us – to you and to me. Today we should examine ourselves on how we respond to the word of God – the divine seed.

The four responses to that word can be four different types of people. The four responses can also be found in each one of us – depending on our own response at different times in our life – childhood, youth, adulthood, old age.

Let us ask God today for the grace to open our hearts and minds to receive God's word with love, affection and understanding. After Jesus finished his sermon on the Bread of Life and the Eucharist in the sixth chapter of St. John's Gospel, the Evangelist says that many of his disciples walked away from him. Sadly, Jesus said to the Twelve, "Do you also wish to go away?" Then Peter answered him, "Lord, to whom shall we go? You have the words of everlasting life."

If we accept his word and live it perseveringly, we also will have everlasting life right now, because God's word is the divine seed of eternal life. We should pray today and tell Jesus: "Lord, I am here before you. Grant that my heart may be the good ground, ready to receive the seed of your divine word, and ready to bring forth abundant fruit of good works." Amen.

QUINQUAGESIMA SUNDAY

Readings: 1 Corinthians 13:1-13; Luke 18:31-43

Suffering and Love

Ash Wednesday this week signals the beginning of Lent, which lasts for forty days, not counting the Sundays. The purpose of Lent is to prepare our minds and hearts to properly celebrate the feast of the Resurrection of Jesus on Easter Sunday. It is a period of prayer and penance in remembrance of Jesus' forty days of fasting in the wilderness as he prepared for his public life.

The Church now requires fasting and abstinence on Ash Wednesday and Good Friday for all adults between the ages of 18 to 59. Abstinence from meat on Fridays is required of all who are fourteen or older. In addition to fast and abstinence, the season of Lent should be penitential in other ways also. Traditional Catholic practices during this time are extra prayer, almsgiving and works of charity. Many try to attend Mass during the week when they can. It is also recommended to give up something one likes such as candy, sweets, alcohol, television, films.

The spiritual purpose of these acts of self-denial is to dispose ourselves for a more fruitful reception of the graces Jesus merited for us by his passion and death on the cross on Calvary. Lent reminds us that we have been redeemed and elevated to the supernatural level by the suffering of Jesus Christ, God made man, and that he suffered for us because he loves us. It reminds us that we were created for Heaven and eternal life, something many tend to forget when they are immersed in earthly concerns. Today I want to highlight two points contained in the readings: suffering and love.

1. We should recall that Jesus freely suffered a most painful death on the cross to atone for all the sins of mankind. What he did no one else could do. Because he is both God and man, his suffering has infinite worth. Suffering is the result of sin. Before the sin of Adam and Eve there was no suffering and no death in the Garden of Eden.

During his public life Jesus predicted three times that he would suffer, die and rise again from the dead according to the prophets. Today's Gospel Reading from Luke presents his third prediction. The twelve Apostles, however, did not understand him. They were expecting a glorious, triumphant Messiah, not a suffering Messiah like Jesus. We also find it hard to understand such a Savior.

We all know what suffering is because we all have suffered, but we may not be able to define suffering. A simple definition is this: Suffering is a painful experience of soul or body that is caused by the presence of some evil or the lack of some good. Examples are physical pain, hunger, thirst, frustration, disappointment, or sorrow at the death of a loved one. Suffering can be both physical and mental. It is always associated with pain of some kind and is the result of sin – either our own sins or the sins of others.

It is hard for us to understand the "why" of suffering. Pope John Paul II wrote a profound letter on suffering called "The Christian Meaning of Suffering" (1984). To give some understanding of suffering, consider the following:

Suffering helps us to atone for our sins, to remind us that we are mere creatures who are totally dependent on God, and also to reduce the time we must spend in purgatory.

It helps us to be able to offer sacrifices to God and to give him the adoration he deserves.

It helps us to unite ourselves with Christ in his sufferings on the cross as an expression of our love for him – and to become more like him who suffered for us.

It helps us to appreciate more deeply what Jesus did for us on Calvary.

2. Why did Jesus suffer and die for us? The simple answer we have in the Bible and in the teaching of the Church is because he loves us, that is, he seeks our good, our joy, our happiness, primarily eternal but also temporal; he suffered for us in order to save us from sin and the anguish of eternal suffering in hell. St. John summarizes it very well in 3:16: "For God so loved the world that he gave his only Son, so that everyone who believes in him may not perish but may have eternal life."

Love of God is the perfection of the law and sums up all the law and the prophets: "You shall love the Lord your God with all your heart, with all yours soul...." In today's Epistle St. Paul sings the praises of charity or love in lyrical terms. He says that love is patient... kind... not envious... not arrogant... not ambitious... not self-seeking... not provoked; thinks no evil... bears all things, believes all things, hopes all things, and endures all things. Charity never fails, but all human things do, including the temporary charismatic gifts of God.

Now we see him in a mirror darkly, then we shall see him as he is – face to face. Faith, hope and charity abide, but the greatest of these is charity. In Heaven for the saints faith and hope will give way to vision and possession – and only charity will remain. So now, faith; then, vision. The charity Paul praises was realized by Jesus in dying for us on the cross.

In passing we might note two kinds of blindness suggested in the Gospel for today. There is the physical blindness of the beggar, and the spiritual blindness of the disciples and the Pharisees.

Conclusion

St. Ignatius Loyola in his *Spiritual Exercises*, in the first meditation on sin, recommends that we kneel before the crucifix and ask ourselves three questions: (1) What have I done for Christ in the past? (2) What am I doing for Christ right now? (3) What ought I to do for Christ?

During this time of Lent we can all profit by asking ourselves these questions and coming up with some concrete answers and firm resolutions for the future. We should make our own the question of the blind beggar to Jesus: "Lord, that I may see!"

FIRST SUNDAY OF LENT

Readings: 2 Corinthians 6:1-10; Matthew 4:1-11

Spiritual Warfare in the Wilderness

Each year on the first Sunday of Lent we reflect on the temptation of Jesus in the wilderness. The conflict is between Jesus and Satan, the Son of God and the devil. It is a case of spiritual warfare in solitude.

The word "satan" means adversary or tempter. That is

what the devil is to Jesus and also to us. Jesus is wholly sinless; in fact, because he is the Son of God he cannot sin – he is impeccable. The devil is God's enemy; he hates God and he hates human beings because we are destined to take his place in Heaven – the place he lost by the first sin of pride and rebellion against God. Satan sees Jesus as a rival and so he tries to turn him into an earthly, material messiah.

In this sermon I will propose three points: temptation, the devil, and how to overcome the devil.

The Temptations of Jesus

Jesus was led by the Holy Spirit into the wilderness to be tempted by the devil. He freely submits himself to temptation. In this he differs from us who are tempted contrary to our will. Jesus' three temptations are like those of Adam and Eve, and also like that of the Israelites in the wilderness. The three are: (1) Lack of trust in God, (2) presumption, and (3) idolatry. Jesus rejects each one and in the process he quotes God's word in the Book of Deuteronomy.

Temptation can be defined as an inducement to sin – an act of the will to prefer self to God, to deliberately violate one of God's commandments. Temptations can come from the world, the flesh, and the devil. Some temptations come from the outside and others come from within us because of concupiscence which is a tendency to sin as a result of the original sin inherited from our first parent, Adam. Everyone is subject to temptation. There is no person or place protected against it. St. Matthew tells us that Jesus was tempted, but it was external and from the devil. Because he was divine and free of concupiscence he could not be tempted from within. God allows temptations to test us like Job, to keep us humble so we can grow in virtue. His grace is always with us and no one is tempted beyond his power to resist. Our main line of defense is prayer, the sacraments, fasting, and almsgiving.

The Tempter – Satan or the Devil

Who is the devil? Why does he tempt us? And where did he come from since everything God made is good and he is bent on evil?

The devil (or Satan or Lucifer) is a fallen angel who is mentioned often in the Bible (Genesis, Job, Gospels, 2 Peter, Jude). Angels are rational, spiritual beings without a body, inferior to God but superior to men – they are pure spirits. They were created good by God but some made themselves evil by rebelling against God. Their sin was pride and when they sinned hell was created for them. We do not know how many there are, but some theologians speculate that about one third of the angels followed Lucifer and rebelled against God. So the devil is real and he is our personal enemy. The devil is not just some impersonal force for evil, as many modern intellectuals seem to hold.

The devil can tempt us by suggesting evil, but he cannot force us to sin. Also, the devil does not know or have access to our inner thoughts, but he knows us well by observing how we speak and act. Like a wise general, he attacks us at our weak points. Note how he first tempted Jesus with food when he was hungry after fasting for forty days.

Each person has his own guardian angel (see Matthew 18:10), but there is no evidence from the Bible or Church tradition that each person has a devil assigned to tempt him. Some holy cards give this impression, when they show a child with an angel whispering into one ear and a devil into the other.

God permits us to be tempted by the devil, but we always have the grace to resist temptation. St. Paul tells us that no one is tempted beyond his power to resist (1 Corinthians 10:13).

Why does God allow the devil to tempt us? This is difficult to understand. Spiritual writers assign at least three reasons: (1) God allows us to be tempted to show his power in defeating the devil, because God's grace is more powerful than all the weapons of the devil; (2) so that we might become more humble, knowing that we need God's help to overcome the devil; and (3) to strengthen us in virtue as a result of the struggle.

In the Bible we see the following contrast: In Genesis the devil tempts Adam and Eve in the Garden of Eden and leads them into sin; in Matthew's Gospel the devil tempts Jesus in the wilderness and is defeated by him.

How to Overcome the Devil

The weapons we need to defeat the devil are well known: prayer, fasting, almsgiving, self-denial, the sacraments, reading the Bible, avoiding the near occasions of sin such as immoral television, videos, music, magazines, books, and Internet pornography. We should know our faith well and be familiar with the Bible, especially the New Testament. Note how Jesus defeats the devil with three quotes from Deuteronomy (chapters 6 and 8).

Conclusion

The purpose of Lent is conversion of heart – turning away from inordinate attachment to creatures and turning to God. May God grant the grace to each one of us to imitate Jesus in the wilderness this Lent – to move a little bit away from our attachment to self and to creatures, and to turn to him with an increase of trust, humility and obedience.

Our prayer should be that of Jesus: (a) "Man does not live by bread alone, but by every word that proceeds from the mouth of God" (Deuteronomy 8:3); (b) "You must not put the Lord your God to the test" (Deuteronomy 6:16); (c) "You shall do homage to the Lord your God; him alone shall you serve" (Deuteronomy 6:13).

At the conclusion of the account, St. Matthew writes: "Then the devil left him; and behold, angels came and ministered to him" (Matthew 4:11). Jesus defeated the devil and shows us how to overcome him.

SECOND SUNDAY OF LENT

Readings: 1 Thessalonians 4:1-7; Matthew 17:1-9

Transfiguration: Encouragement for Lent

On the Second Sunday of Lent the Church gives us a glimpse of the glory and divinity of Jesus in his transfiguration on Mount Tabor in Galilee. The word "transfiguration" means to undergo a change of figure or appearance. Fr. John Hardon defines it as "the glorification of the appearance of Jesus with intense light before his resurrection" (*Dictionary*, p. 544). In this mystery we find a summons to put faith and hope in Jesus – and to strive for holiness, to become more like him.

The top of Mount Tabor is about 1000 feet above the valley of Esdraelon in northern Galilee. Jesus climbs the mountain accompanied by Peter, James and John, the same disciples he will take with him to witness his agony in the Garden of Gethsemane. His purpose is to pray and also to manifest some of his divine glory to them. This takes place just six days after his first prediction of his passion and death, as related in Matthew (16:21ff.).

Jesus wants his disciples to see him transfigured in order to strengthen them for the coming passion so that they will not lose faith in him. Jesus reveals his divinity to them: (1) by letting it shine through his humanity – his face glowed like the sun and his clothes became white as snow; (2) by bringing back from the dead Moses and Elijah as witnesses to him. Moses represents the Law and Elijah the prophets. Their presence with Jesus is another proof of the immortality of the soul and eternal life. They spoke to him of his "departure," his Passover from this life to the Father. Here we find another indication that everything in the Old Testament points to Christ in one way or another. He reveals his divinity to them (3) by evoking the awe inspiring testimony of the Father when the voice booms out of the cloud: "This is my beloved Son on whom my favor rests. Listen to him." In the Old Testament the cloud is a visible sign of God's presence.

What is the meaning of the Transfiguration of Jesus? It means that Jesus is predicting or foreshadowing his coming triumph – his resurrection and victory over sin and death. This is the promise; the disciples must believe and hope in him alone. The Transfiguration, therefore, strengthens them for their coming apostolate – an apostolate of witness, suffering and death for the sake of Christ. Thus, there is a close link between Tabor and Calvary.

Another aspect of the Transfiguration is that Jesus gives his three disciples a foretaste of Heaven, but rejects Peter's desire to remain in it now before the testing. The process here is one of going through suffering to glory: the cross first, and then the crown.

The Church presents the mystery of the Transfiguration to us on the Second Sunday of Lent each year for a number of reasons: (1) to strengthen us in our resolve to share the cross of Jesus; (2) to cheer us up and encourage us amid the rigors of Lent, which formerly was forty days of fasting, by showing us some of Jesus' glory – the promise of which will be ours if we are faithful to our call; (3) to prepare us for the future trials.

In our following of Christ we must walk the way of suffering to glory, just as he did. He tells us in St. Luke's Gospel to take up our cross *daily* and follow him. Also, Jesus said to the two disciples on the road to Emmaus: "Ought not the Christ to have suffered and so enter into his glory?" (Luke 24:26). The Transfiguration was meant for the disciples at the time: "Do not tell anyone of the vision until the Son of Man has risen from the dead" (Matthew 17:9). But it surely contains a message for all followers of Christ.

Conclusion

Our Lord leads us on the way to eternal life and goes before us. By reflecting on his glorious Transfiguration we should be encouraged to continue our practice of self-denial during this Lent – whatever we have chosen to do: fasting, giving up sweets or alcohol or television or whatever.

Peter, James and John were emboldened to give their whole lives to Christ – to the shedding of their blood. We should remember that Jesus is always with us to help us with his grace. And victory is certain if we remain faithful to him.

I conclude with those powerful words of the Father from the bright cloud, which should give us courage to imitate Jesus: "This is my beloved Son in whom I am well pleased. Listen to him" – and do what he tells you. To each one of us he says, "Listen to him – and do what he tells you." If you do that, your life will be a success – here and hereafter.

THIRD SUNDAY OF LENT

Readings: Ephesians 5:1-9; Luke 11:14-28

Now You Are Light in the Lord

There is a culture war raging in our society between secular humanism (making man a god) and belief in Jesus Christ and the one true God. The battle is between Jesus Christ and Satan, between darkness and light. No one is preserved from it. It is everywhere – in the media, in schools and universities, in the government, in business and even in the Church. The war is between those who believe in God, the Father Almighty, Creator of Heaven and earth – and those who do not believe. They set up some creature as a god – the State usually, but also money and power.

St. Paul says in today's Epistle from Ephesians, "You were once darkness, but now you are light in the Lord. Walk then as children of light." Darkness here means living in sin without the grace of Christ, especially for those without Baptism who are immersed in error, evil, injustice and death. Light stands for the grace of Baptism, divine revelation and the truth of God; it also means goodness, justice, virtue, life and love.

St. Paul urges us to avoid being "children of darkness," that is, living in the power of the devil and error regarding God, man and the world. He urges us to be "children of light," that is, living in grace, in Christ, in the Lord, and avoiding all sin. St. Paul mentions various kinds of immorality that exclude one from the kingdom of God, such as uncleanness, fornication, covetousness and idolatry. His counsel is that we should "Walk as children of light, for the fruit of light is in all goodness, justice and truth."

Two weeks ago on the First Sunday of Lent we saw Jesus in a struggle with the devil. Satan was the aggressor. In today's reading we see Jesus on the offensive against the devil. He drives him out of the sick man and in doing so attacks the whole kingdom of Satan. In today's reading Jesus tells us what it means to "walk in the light" and to "walk as children of the light." He challenges us to be faithful to him – to be loyal to him in all circumstances of our daily life.

Jesus is the "stronger one" who binds the strong one, that is, the devil. Jesus is in the process of defeating the devil by his passion, death and resurrection. We must be careful not to lose the grace of God. If we do, our last state could be worse than our first state without his grace.

The model Christian in this regard is his holy Mother who is praised in the last verse of the Gospel Reading: "Rather, blessed are they who hear the word of God and keep it." Mary did that perfectly all her life and especially in her answer to the Archangel Gabriel: "Let it be done to me according to your word."

American society is rapidly becoming more secular, atheistic and immoral. This anti-Christian ideology is being promoted in the media, in our schools, in our courts of law. They are promoting sexual immorality of all kinds: abortion, homosexuality and same-sex marriage. As Catholics we should oppose this ideology in any way we can. We should avoid immorality of all kinds and give good example by our practice of love of God and neighbor. In fulfilling our civic duty, we should vote for candidates of integrity who are committed to defending God, country and family. Those who do that are the "children of light" whom St. Paul talks about because they are walking in truth and goodness.

Conclusion

The only clear beacon of light in the darkness of the world is the Catholic Church, which is the Body of Christ and which proclaims the whole Gospel of Jesus Christ. He is the light of the world and he sheds his light on us through his Church. If we remain faithful to him – to his teaching and his Church – we will not be in the darkness of sin and error, we will not be under the power of the devil, but we will walk as children of light in truth and goodness. If we persevere, and we will if we rely on his grace, we will share in his eternal life with the saints and martyrs.

If we keep his commandments, he will abide in us as in a temple, and we will "walk in love" as St. Paul urges us in today's Epistle. Rooted in his truth and love, with the power of his grace we will triumph over the devil just as Jesus did. Jesus promised us victory: "Take courage! I have overcome the world" (John 16:33).

FOURTH SUNDAY OF LENT

Readings: Galatians 4:22-31; John 6:1-15

Rejoice, O Jerusalem

"Rejoice, O Jerusalem, and come together all of you who love her. Rejoice... and be filled with the abundance of delights" (Introit). Today, the Fourth Sunday of Lent, is called "Laetare Sunday" because of the first word in the Introit in

Latin, which means "rejoice." It is also the halfway point in the forty days of Lent.

What are the "delights" the prophet speaks about? The answer is found in today's Gospel Reading that Jesus is the Bread of Life. The Mass today presents a sense of joy at having reached the middle of Lent, which is a time of prayer, fasting and almsgiving. We rejoice because we know that Easter will soon be here. Then we will rejoice with the Risen Lord and Mary and the Apostles in the Upper Room. The time of penance and self-denial will soon be over. Jesus, the Bread of Life, is the cause of our joy.

In the Epistle St. Paul contrasts the old Law of Moses with the new law of Christ. He sees it as the difference between slavery and freedom – symbolized by the two wives of Abraham: Hagar and Sarah. In Paul's interpretation of Scripture, Hagar stands for Mt. Sinai and the Mosaic Law with its 613 serious laws to be observed; it also refers to those who refuse to believe in Jesus. Sarah stands for the New Jerusalem from Heaven, that is, the Church which is the mother of many children. The Church grows in spite of persecution, for example in China, Korea and Africa. We rejoice today because we have been chosen to be members of his Church and heirs of Heaven.

The Gospel recalls the beautiful story of the miraculous feeding of 5,000 men with only five loaves and two fish. The evangelists considered this miracle so important that it is the only one recorded in all four Gospels. It demonstrates the divine power of Jesus and St. John says it is a sign (6:14). A sign of what? It is a sign of his divinity and that Jesus is the promised Messiah. This miracle reminds us of the miraculous manna in the desert which sustained the wandering Israelites for forty years. Because of his infinite power, God can create new things out of nothing; he can change one thing into another, as Jesus changed water into delicious wine at the Marriage Feast of Cana.

The miracle of the loaves and fishes foreshadows Holy

Thursday, when Jesus will institute the Mass and the Blessed Sacrament with his Real Presence under the appearances of bread and wine. The implicit argument runs like this: If Jesus can multiply bread to eat, he can also change ordinary bread and wine into his own Body and Blood.

That is what happens during the Holy Sacrifice of the Mass. The Mass is the heart and soul of Catholicism. Without the Mass there is no Catholic Church, no hierarchy, no priests, no sacraments. Bishops and priests are ministers of the word and the sacraments. Catholic churches are built in such a way that the main focus is on the altar where the Mass is celebrated.

The Mass is a sacrifice in the sense that it re-presents, or presents again, in an unbloody or sacramental way the unique sacrifice of Jesus on Calvary. There is only one sacrifice, that of Jesus, and its merits are infinite because he is God Almighty in the flesh. The primary purpose of the Mass is to give glory to God; the secondary purpose is the salvation of men through communion with Christ who is the Bread of Life.

The Holy Eucharist is a sacrament which means that it is a sacred sign instituted by Christ to signify grace and to communicate it to us. So the manna in the desert of the Old Testament and the multiplication of the loaves by Jesus find their final fulfillment in the Holy Eucharist.

One result of the Mass is the Blessed Sacrament in the tabernacle with the Real Presence of Jesus under the appearances of bread and wine as our friend and companion. We can visit him any time and pour out our hearts to him in personal prayer. Since we all partake of the one body of Christ and so share in his divine life, we become members of the Mystical Body of Christ and form one Church, just as many grains of wheat make one loaf of bread and many grapes one glass of wine.

During this period of Lent we should try to receive the Lord often in Holy Communion, go to confession, practice some self-denial, and visit him in the Blessed Sacrament – he is always there for us. He says to us: "Come to me all you who are heavily burdened and I will give you rest.... For my yoke is easy, and my burden is light" (Matthew 11:28 & 30). You can also make what is called a "spiritual communion" by desiring to receive him if it were possible. It is reported of St. Francis de Sales that he did that every fifteen minutes.

The Israelites in the desert lived on the manna for about forty years. We live spiritually through eating the Body of Christ in Holy Communion. Jesus said in John 6:53-54: "Amen, amen I say to you, unless you eat the flesh of the Son of Man and drink his blood, you do not have life in you. Whoever eats my flesh and drinks my blood has eternal life, and I will raise him up on the last day." Those are truly words of hope.

Conclusion

Finally, on Laetare Sunday, because we have hope in Jesus and the resurrection of the body, we rejoice. We rejoice also because we know we have been freed from sin by Christ (first reading) and are moving with Jesus towards the heavenly Jerusalem, which is eternal life.

FIFTH SUNDAY OF LENT – PASSION SUNDAY

Readings: Hebrews 9:11-15; John 8:46-59

Sin Causes Suffering

Today, the Fifth Sunday of Lent, is called "Passion Sunday" because, during the next two weeks before Easter, the liturgy concentrates on the suffering and death of Jesus to atone for our sins. During this time we recall and meditate on all the things the Lord Jesus suffered for our sake. It is a time of mourning, rather than rejoicing. It is a time of preparation for the joys of Easter. Jesus is our High Priest or Mediator, our Go-Between – between the all-holy God and us poor sinners. A key point that runs through this liturgy is the causal connection between sin and suffering.

If we ask, "Why did Jesus have to suffer?" the simple answer is that he offered himself to the Father to make satisfaction for the sins of mankind.

Let us now consider briefly that little but important word "sin." Sin is defined as an offense against God. It is something like a serious offense against one's father or mother. Sin is the greatest evil in the world because God is infinite goodness. We divide sins into mortal and venial. A mortal sin is a serious offense against God which results in the loss of sanctifying grace. It makes one an enemy of God and deserving of eternal punishment in hell. Examples are blasphemy, sacrilege, murder, adultery, fornication, homosexual activity, and so forth.

A venial sin is a minor offense against God that does not cause a loss of grace, but it does weaken it and, if deliberate, can lead the way to mortal sin. Examples would be white lies of convenience, gossip, rudeness, rash judgment of others.

In order to gain forgiveness of mortal sins one must be sorry and have purpose of amendment, make a good confession to a priest, and then do the penance imposed by the confessor. The result is regaining grace and reconciliation with God. The temporal punishment due to sin in purgatory is diminished in this life by prayer, penance, almsgiving and gaining indulgences.

Since sin is an offense against an infinite God, man who is finite cannot satisfy for it by himself – it is too much for him. So after the original sin of Adam and Eve in Paradise, and the personal sins of individuals, there was a need of a redeemer, a mediator who could adequately atone for the sins of mankind. Jesus Christ is that Mediator, Redeemer and High Priest, as we read in today's Epistle from the Letter to the Hebrews.

The ritual of the Old Testament involved the shedding of the blood of animals to atone for sins, but it was not adequate – it produced only what is called "ritual cleanness." Jesus Christ, God and man, is the perfect High Priest who atones, with his own blood, for the sins of all mankind. His sacrifice merits grace for all and cleans consciences. Because he is God in the flesh, his grace is infinite and is applied to us through the sacraments of the Church.

These two weeks before Easter are called "Passiontide" which means a time of suffering. The Church urges us to remember and think about Jesus' suffering for us. Suffering itself is an experience of evil. It is something we all hate and try to avoid. But it is unavoidable in this mortal life because of the constant presence of sin. We suffer something every day – either physical or mental, from ourselves or from others. This is a result of original sin and often our own sins. Passiontide and Holy Week remind us that we were redeemed by suffering – by the suffering of the God-Man, and that we must follow and imitate him.

It is clear from the whole New Testament that Jesus came into this world of time and space to suffer and to make satisfaction for sins. So again there is an essential connection between sin and suffering. If there were no sin, we would not need a redeemer and God would not have become man. Adam and Eve did not need a redeemer before they sinned. Since Jesus is God, his suffering has infinite value, as I said before, and he could satisfy for all the sins of the human race.

The divinity of Jesus is brought out in today's Gospel Reading from John when he says, "Before Abraham was, I am." The Hebrew for "I am" is the name of God – Yahweh. Many think that sin is caused by suffering, for example, that poverty causes crime. That is not true; the reality is the other way around. Sin is followed by suffering – either sooner or later, either in this life or in the next life. As a result of the sin of Adam and Eve, they were expelled from the Garden of Eden and became subject to sickness, suffering and death.

The liar loses his good name; the violent will suffer violence; the sexually promiscuous get deadly diseases.

Because of the love of Jesus for us and what he has done for us, if we live a good life and die in the state of grace, Heaven is open and we can be eternally happy with God. Therefore, Jesus has given meaning to human suffering. He has made it meritorious if accepted for the love of God.

We all have to suffer, whether we want to or not. We all have to die. There is no escape. The point is to make our suffering salvific – to offer it up to God in union with Christ for our own salvation and that of others.

Conclusion

We are Christians, that is, followers of Christ. He says, "If you wish to be my disciples, take up your cross daily and follow me." These words are addressed to you and to me. St. Luke tells us in Acts 5:41 that the Apostles were scourged for preaching Jesus and that they rejoiced that they could suffer something for him. They found joy in their suffering because they saw meaning in it. They were sharing in the sufferings of Christ and had hope of eternal salvation. So during this Passiontide let us thank our Lord for what he has done for us and ask him for the grace to imitate him, to be more like him in bearing the sufferings that come our way each day.

PALM SUNDAY

Readings: Philippians 2:5-11; Matthew 26:36-75; 27:1-54

Christian Paradoxes

G.K. Chesterton once observed that Christianity is full of paradoxes. A paradox is an apparent contradiction – a statement which seems at first to be absurd, but in fact it is well founded. A few examples would be that Jesus is both God and Man, Mary is both virgin and mother, eternal happiness is obtained through suffering, and the Messiah is a meek and humble king.

Today is Palm Sunday when we celebrate the triumphal entry of Jesus into Jerusalem. It is not difficult to imagine the scene of Jesus, riding on a donkey, entering the holy city in triumph as King and Messiah. At the time waving palms was a sign of victory and triumph. The crowd meant it in a political sense, but in the full sense of the Bible it signifies Jesus' victory over sin and death. The kings of the past had entered the city this way – down the Mount of Olives and then up into and through the Golden Gate. Previously Jesus had forbidden his disciples to proclaim him publicly. Now that he is about to die he allows them to honor him openly as Messiah and King. He now accepts recognition as a king, but he is a humble and meek king riding on a peaceful donkey. At the time the people did not understand clearly his divine kingship.

Palm Sunday is the beginning of his glorification, which leads through suffering and death to his resurrection. It is now his hour which he had predicted at least three times. Note the fickleness of the crowd: some of the same individuals who are shouting "Hosanna" in five days will shout "crucify him."

The Mass today brings us fully into the theme of the passion during Holy Week. Why is Jesus so submissive, so meek and humble? There is only one reason – love, love for the Father and love for mankind whom he wants to reconcile with the Father. Isaiah says in chapter 50 that he was wounded for our offenses and by his wounds we were healed. Only infinite love can explain the suffering and humiliation accepted by the Son of God. This is reflected in today's Epistle from the Letter to the Philippians where St. Paul expresses both the divinity and the humanity of Jesus. In the Passion we see the true humanity of Jesus, while his divinity hides itself and almost seems to abandon him. Jesus, who is both human and divine, suffers in his human nature. But from extreme humiliation springs his highest exaltation: "Because of this God highly exalted him…" (Philippians 2:10-11).

To suffer means to endure harm and pain that threatens life in some way. Human suffering requires consciousness and awareness of what is happening. We all wonder why we have to suffer. Suffering is part of God's mysterious plan (see Ephesians and Colossians) that our redemption should be accomplished by the suffering and death of Jesus Christ. Suffering counters our pride. It reminds man of his limitations and that he is a mere creature. Minerals and plants cannot suffer because they have no awareness; animals suffer, but it is different from human suffering because they cannot anticipate the future.

On the cross Jesus attains the high point of his mission into the world. It is his "hour" for which he longed. It is the moment of his glorification which he had predicted: "When I am lifted up from the earth, I will draw all men to myself" (John 12:32). Here we also meet the mysterious "necessity" or "ought" of the cross that Jesus mentions on Easter Sunday evening in his words to his astonished Apostles in the Upper Room (Luke 24:26).

The problem and power of sin is a major theme of the Bible. The mission of Jesus is to destroy the power of sin and death. We only really know what sin is when we contemplate Jesus on the cross and understand what is happening there: God in his human nature suffering and dying to save us from sin and death.

To be human means to suffer. To deal with this we need courage, but courage alone is not enough. We should look to Jesus as our example or model in enduring suffering. Note his humility and his obedience to the Father. He tells us to take up our cross daily and to follow him. We are called "to fill up what is lacking in the suffering of Christ," as St. Paul puts it in Colossians 1:24. If we are true Christians, we must embrace what Christ embraced.

Conclusion

As we look at Jesus on the cross we confront the mystery of suffering and death and the paradox that suffering with Jesus leads to glory and happiness. It is summed up in the expression "the cross and the crown," or glory through suffering. Our task now while we have time is to follow him, to know him through prayer, the sacraments and the study of the Bible. We need only to trust in him and he will give us the strength we need to remain faithful. As he said to his Apostles the day before his passion, "You will have trouble in the world. But have confidence – I have overcome the world" (John 16:33) and "I am with you all days, even unto the end of the world" (Matthew 28:20).

HOLY THURSDAY

Readings: 1 Corinthians 11:20-26; John 13:1-15

Gift of Love

Holy Thursday is also called "Maundy Thursday." Maundy is the French word for the Latin "Mandatum" which means "command." The reason for this is that at the Last Supper Jesus commanded his disciples to love one another as he loved us. Today the Church commemorates three events in Jesus' life: (1) the Mass and the Eucharist; (2) institution of the priesthood; (3) the new commandment of Jesus of mutual love. He gave an example of the latter by washing the feet of his twelve Apostles. He taught us by both his words and his deeds.

Jesus instituted the Eucharist in order to make present to all future generations his unique sacrifice of the Cross on Calvary, through which he merited the grace of salvation for all men. He also did it in order to be present with us until the end of the world in the Blessed Sacrament.

The Eucharist is a concrete sign of Jesus' love for us. It is an unbloody re-presentation of his bloody sacrifice on Good Friday. By eating his Body and Blood hidden under the appearances of bread and wine, we unite ourselves with him who is the source of our salvation. We also have him present in the tabernacle on the altar so we can visit him any time.

The primary purpose of the Mass is the glorification of God. The secondary purpose is the salvation and sanctification of mankind, especially of those who attend Mass and worthily receive him in Holy Communion. It is important to remember that when we receive Jesus sacramentally in Communion we also receive the Father and the Holy Spirit in a spiritual way, since in all works outside of the inner life of the Trinity the three Persons are involved.

At the Last Supper Jesus also instituted the priesthood of the New Testament when he said to his Apostles, "Do this in remembrance of me." He instituted the priesthood to make present for all time his sacrifice and his presence with his faithful followers. Without the priesthood there would be no sacraments and no Church. Bishops and priests who have received the Sacrament of Holy Orders are successors of the Apostles and ministers of Jesus' word and his sacraments. He gave them power to forgive sins when he said to them on Easter Sunday after breathing on them, "Whose sins you shall forgive, they are forgiven; whose sins you shall retain, they are retained" (John 20:23).

The third mystery we commemorate on Holy Thursday is Jesus' commandment to love one another as he has loved us. How has he loved us? With infinite love which moved him to become man for us. As a sign of his love and humility, he washes the feet of his Apostles – a task that was normally done by slaves. Then he said, "I have given you an example; you are to do as I have done to you" (John 13:15).

Jesus commands us to love one another and to serve each other. This law of charity is the basis of a truly Christian society. We love one another first of all by keeping the Commandments – all ten of them, and respecting the rights of every person. In a truly Christian society there is no need of a large police force to compel people to respect the rights of others because they all keep the Commandments. Peace is first in the heart and then in relations with others.

Pope John Paul II often defined love as the "self-gift" of one person to another. That is what our Blessed Lord does for us in the Holy Eucharist – he gives himself to us and invites us to give ourselves to him – with faith, hope and charity.

Conclusion

Our Response today should be an attitude of thanksgiving to Jesus for all he has done for us – for his merciful love for us. Our hearts should be moved at the sight of what he has done for us. Now is the time to return love for love, to try harder to get along with relatives and friends, to try harder every day to practice love of God and love of neighbor. Today Jesus is saying to each one of us – to you and to me: "A new commandment I give to you, that you love one another, even as I have loved you, that you also love one another" (John 13:34).

HOLY SATURDAY

Readings: Colossians 3:1-4; Matthew 28:1-7

Glorification

The ancient liturgy of Holy Saturday presents before our eyes and ears the whole history of salvation which culminates in Christ's Easter mystery – his glorious resurrection from the dead. It also becomes the history of each human being through Baptism which inserts him into this mystery. That is why water and Baptism are so emphasized in tonight's liturgy.

Thus our Lord himself, the light of the world, is presented to us under the sign of the Paschal Candle. For, he has scattered the darkness of our sins by the grace of his light.

Then the solemn praise of Easter (*Exultet*) is sung, describing the splendor of the holy night of the resurrection.

Following this, God's mighty works in the Old Testament are commemorated, which are pale images or symbols of the wonders of Jesus and the New Testament: creation of the world, the call of Abraham and Isaac, the Passover, the crossing of the Red Sea where the water is a symbol of Baptism, the call of the prophets Isaiah and Ezekiel.

Then the water of Baptism is blessed in which, buried with Christ we die to sin and we rise again with him to walk in a new life free from sin (Romans 6:4).

Then we engage ourselves by renewing our baptismal promises in order to bear witness in all our life to the grace which Christ merited for us by his death and conferred on us at our Baptism.

Finally, after imploring the prayers of all the saints – the Church triumphant in Heaven – we conclude the sacred vigil with the Mass of the Resurrection.

The Holy Week Triduum is the most sacred liturgy of the whole year. To celebrate Easter means to "pass over" with Christ from death to life, that is, from sin to grace and holiness of life that leads finally to eternal life with God. It is a "passage" begun with our Baptism, which must be carried out in an ever fuller way during our whole life. Baptism is participation in Christ's death and it means crucifying the "old man," that is, the man of sin that resides in us as a result of original sin. It means dying "to sin, once for all with him" (Romans 6:10). To baptized Christians St. Paul says, "You must consider yourself dead to sin, and alive to God in Christ Jesus" (Romans 6:11).

When Jesus died on Calvary, his body was placed in the tomb. But what about his soul? As we say in the Apostles

Creed, "He descended into hell," that is, to the underworld which the Jews of the time called "sheol." His soul was there about 38 hours, from Friday at 3 p.m. until Sunday morning about 4 or 5 a.m. There he met and set free all the saints who died before Christ and led them into Heaven. Catholic tradition often calls that place the "limbo of the Fathers."

Conclusion

In the *Breviary* or *Divine office* for Holy Saturday there is a beautiful reading from an ancient homily for Holy Saturday. It presents a conversation in the underworld between Jesus and Adam, and in a way summarizes the liturgy of Holy Saturday. [The preacher may conclude this homily by reading the passage from Volume II, pp. 320-322.]

EASTER SUNDAY

Readings: 1 Corinthians 5:7-8; Mark 16:1-8

Rejoice!

On Easter Sunday we celebrate the resurrection of Jesus from the dead. The Church urges us today to rejoice, using the words of the Psalmist in the Gradual (118:24), "This is the day the Lord has made; let us rejoice and be glad in it." We rejoice in the truth of the resurrection which is the foundation of our Christian hope of eternal life.

What is the reason for rejoicing on Easter Sunday? The reason is basic, fundamental: By his resurrection Jesus has triumphed over sin, and death which is the result of sin. Adam lost grace and immortality by his sin; Jesus restored it by his death and resurrection. But his triumph is not just for himself. It is also for us and for all who believe in him, are baptized, and receive his sacraments. As Jesus said, "I am the resurrection and the life; he who believes in me, even though he be dead, shall live" (John 11:25). Through our faith, baptism, and divine grace we are united to him and are members of his Mystical Body. So what happens to him happens to us also, since we live by his life.

Now we share in his triumph in a beginning way by possessing his grace, the supernatural life of the soul. If we die in his grace, we will be united with him forever and we will also rise from the dead as he did. Jesus assures us of this in John 6:54: "He who eats my flesh and drinks my blood has eternal life, and I will raise him up on the last day."

In the Epistle for today St. Paul tells us "to purge out the old leaven (= yeast), that you may be a new dough, as you really are without leaven." For the Jews of the time leaven or yeast was thought to be a symbol of corruption, so they ate only unleavened bread at Passover. By getting rid of leaven Paul means to reject all sin and we do that by sincere prayer, contrition for our sins, and making a good confession. It is a call to a life of holiness, a call to strive to be a saint.

Paul says that the Christian is "a new dough," that is, "a new creature" made in the image of Christ, who is now reconciled to God through Christ. In other words, this means that, by rejecting sin and embracing Christ, we are made into new creatures by baptism and grace.

The Gospel Reading today from the last chapter of St. Mark gives a very brief account of the resurrection. The women found the tomb empty – the body of Jesus was not there. They were astonished and afraid. Here we see that Jesus' disciples did not yet believe in the resurrection, even though he had predicted it several times. The women saw an angel who told them, "He is risen; he is not here." Several other appearances of the glorified Christ are reported in Matthew, Luke and John.

After his resurrection from the dead Jesus began a new glorified life at the right hand of the Father. While he was dead, and his soul was separated from his body, his soul went to the underworld or the Limbo of the Fathers and set free all the saints of the Old Testament from Adam to John the Baptist and St. Joseph. We commemorated this mystery yesterday on Holy Saturday.

The resurrection of Jesus gives us hope and joy, two themes that run through the Easter Season. Jesus says to each one of us, "I have entered into eternal life and you will too, if you follow me." Hope means that we expect to receive some good thing in the future. Natural hope means that we will attain that good by our own efforts or by some good luck; supernatural hope means that we will attain it with the help of God and by the infinite power of God. So we hope to share in the resurrection of Jesus by the power of God.

Christ therefore is our hope. And hope gives rise to a sense of joy which is the emotion connected with the attainment of some good. Therefore, the Church says to us today: Rejoice! "This is the day the Lord has made; let us rejoice and be glad in it." We rejoice because Jesus has triumphed over sin and death and we will too if we remain united to him.

The angel in the white robe said to the terrified women: "He is risen. He is not here," that is, he is now glorified at the right hand of the Father where he lives forever to make intercession for you. May God bless you and may you have a truly joyful Easter because you believe and realize that the Lord is truly risen.

Conclusion

"This is the day the Lord has made. Let us rejoice and be glad in it." Amen.

LOW SUNDAY – DIVINE MERCY SUNDAY

Readings: 1 John 5:4-10; John 20:19-31

Peace Be With You!

The First Sunday after Easter has been known for centuries as "Low Sunday" because it comes after the "High" feast of Easter. It is also known as "Sunday in White Robes" (Latin = *Dominica in Albis*) because the newly baptized Christians at Easter in the early Church put aside the white robe they wore for a week. More recently it has been called "Divine Mercy Sunday" to recall the revelation given to St. Faustina in the 1930s.

"Peace be with you." These are Jesus' first words to his disciples after his resurrection. "Peace be with you." Jesus communicates his peace to his followers and to all believers. It is his to give because he has reconciled us to the Father by his death for our sins.

In his discourse at the Last Supper Jesus had said, "Peace I leave with you, my peace I give to you; not as the world gives do I give to you." The reason for this is that his peace makes us friends and even children of God.

What is peace? It is more than the absence of war or conflict. Peace means the tranquility of order. It means to be in harmony with all things. It means well-being, serenity, completeness and rest. So peace is the state of the person who lives in harmony with God, with his neighbor and with himself. In Hebrew the word is "Shalom."

What is the source of peace? Peace results from doing God's will and avoiding all sin. It results from possessing divine grace and the Holy Spirit. Peace is one of the twelve fruits of the Holy Spirit (see Galatians 5:22-23). Being in the state of grace means that we are friends of God. In fact, we are his children and heirs of Heaven. It means that we are free from sin and the consequences of sin. The poet Dante said in his *Paradiso*, "His will is our peace."

What is the enemy of peace? Simply, it is mortal sin because mortal sin makes us enemies of God and puts us in conflict with our neighbor. The prophet Isaiah said, "There is no peace for the wicked" (Isaiah 48:22).

Jesus is "The Prince of Peace" because he reconciles us to God and with one another. In today's Gospel Reading he says three times, "Peace be with you." Peace obviously is a key reality in the thinking of Jesus.

The peace which Jesus wished for his apostles and for us is threefold: (1) peace with God; (2) peace with our neighbor; (3) peace with our selves.

Peace with God is most important and the other forms flow from that. It means doing God's will in all things, avoiding all sin, and being in the state of grace. God dwells in the heart of the one who does his will. As Jesus said, "Those who love me will keep my word, and my Father will love them, and we will come to them and make our home with them" (John 14:23).

Peace with our neighbor is the result of avoiding sins like lying, coveting the goods of others, killing, abortion, stealing, adultery, envy. These sins produce conflict with others and destroy any true peace.

Peace with our selves consists in the twofold subjection of our passions to reason, and our reason to God. A person carried away by anger or avarice or pride or lust cannot be at peace with himself. When reason is subject to God, then the passions can be controlled and made subject to reason. If we always strive to do God's will, then our passions will be subject to our will.

Conclusion

Jesus wishes us peace. His "Peace be with you" is directed not just to his apostles, but also to each one of us. If we have faith in him and do his will, we will live in peace, no matter what happens in the world or in Church politics. As he said to Thomas, "Blessed are those who have not seen, and yet have believed" (John 20:29).

For our part, we should try, according to our state in life, to spread the peace of Christ to those we live with and encounter daily. In short, we should try to be ambassadors of peace. Those who do that are blessed and are living the Beatitude: "Blessed are the peacemakers for they shall be called the children of God."

May the grace and peace of our Lord Jesus Christ, the love of God, and the fellowship of the Holy Spirit be with all of you. Amen.

SECOND SUNDAY AFTER EASTER

Readings: 1 Peter 2:21-25; John 10:11-16

The Good Shepherd

The Second Sunday after Easter is called "Good Shepherd Sunday" because of the Gospel Reading from St. John. Jesus is the Good Shepherd and we are the sheep of his flock. He is therefore our divine Pastor, which is another name for shepherd. We are dealing here with a comparison or an analogy, that is, just as a good shepherd cares for his sheep, so also does Jesus care for us and our spiritual well-being.

The good shepherd feeds his flock, defends them with his life, guides them to green pastures, knows each one individually, loves them and calls each one by a name. The sheep, on their part, know their shepherd, trust him and follow him. Jesus is saying to us in today's reading that he has the same love and care for us that the good shepherd has for his flock.

As city dwellers in America most of us have no personal experience of shepherds and sheep as Jesus and his listeners did. So it is perhaps difficult for us to appreciate the full meaning of the comparison between the good shepherd and his sheep and Jesus to us.

The point here is that Jesus feeds and protects his flock, namely us, with divine truth and the Eucharist as food for our souls. In the epistle St. Peter says that Jesus is "the shepherd and guardian of our souls." He feeds and protects us by the teaching of his Church, the seven sacraments, and his word of revelation contained in the Bible. For our part, as members of his flock, we should obey the Vicar of Christ because as the Chief Shepherd representing Jesus he is the principle of unity of the Church.

The good shepherd protects his sheep and is ready to lay down his life for them. That is what Jesus did for us on Calvary when he offered his life in atonement for our sins and the sins of the whole world. Those who follow him closely, those who imitate him will also have to suffer with him.

St. Peter says that "Christ suffered for us" (1 Peter 2:21). By his death Jesus has taken away the guilt of our sins, if we repent and confess them. But there remains the temporal punishment due to sin which must be endured in purgatory. By our prayers and good works we can gain indulgences for the souls in purgatory. Indulgences effect the remission of the sufferings of purgatory and are either partial or plenary. The Church attaches indulgences to certain prayers and devotions, such as the Rosary said before the Blessed Sacrament, the Stations of the Cross, reading the Bible and so forth.

The conditions for gaining a plenary indulgence, or the complete remission of the pains of purgatory for one soul, are: (1) the intention to gain the indulgence; (2) doing the work, for example, praying the Rosary before the Blessed Sacrament, (3) Holy Communion on that day; (4) confession eight days before or after the good work; 5) no attachment to sin. If something is lacking in these conditions, then the person gains a partial indulgence. In one way or another, priests can and do gain indulgences every day.

We must beware of "instant canonization" of good Catholics at their funeral. A result of this is that people do not pray for the deceased, thinking they are already in Heaven. This happened some years ago in the case of a very holy woman whom the priest declared to be a saint at her funeral and said she was in Heaven. This made her daughter happy and for fourteen years she said no prayers for her mother and offered no Masses for the repose of her soul. Then one day she happened to read a pamphlet on purgatory and came to the realization that her mother might be in purgatory and she had done nothing to help her for fourteen years. Immediately she began to pray and earn indulgences for her mother.

Our Lord says that the hirelings flee at the sight of danger. Hirelings are people in authority who are not good shepherds. They do not protect and feed the flock. Their primary concern is their own pleasure and advantage. There have been some sad examples of this in the Church during the past forty years. The wolves are dissenters and heretics both inside and outside the Church. Examples would be Catholic politicians who are pro-abortion and dissenters who say that the Church should change her doctrine on contraception, abortion, homosexuality and the ordination of women to the priesthood.

Just as the good shepherd knows his sheep, so also Jesus knows us perfectly as he knows the Father and the Father knows him. We know him through faith, prayer, sacraments and the Bible. Vatican II reminds us that "Ignorance of Scripture is ignorance of Christ."

Jesus also says that he has other sheep that are not of this fold: "They shall hear my voice, and there shall be one flock and one shepherd." This means that Christ's call or invitation goes out to all mankind. St. Paul says the same thing in 1 Timothy 2:4, "God desires the salvation of men and that all come to the knowledge of the truth." So the Church is missionary by her very nature. A great missionary was

Archbishop Fulton J. Sheen. He died in 1979 but he is still converting people through his books, CDs and videos. All are called to belong to the one Church of Christ so that there may be "one fold and one shepherd."

Conclusion

Let us listen to the invitation Jesus addresses to each one of us; and when possible, we should explain our Catholic faith to others who are searching for God. Listen to the beautiful words of Psalm 23:

> The Lord is my shepherd, I shall not want:
> He makes me lie down in green pastures.
> He leads me beside still waters; he restores my soul.
> He leads me in paths of righteousness for his
> name's sake.
> Even though I walk through the valley of the
> shadow of death,
> I fear no evil, for thou art with me;
> thy rod and thy staff they comfort me.
> Thou preparest a table before me
> in the presence of my enemies;
> Thou anointest my head with oil,
> my cup overflows.
> Surely goodness and mercy shall follow me
> all the days of my life;
> and I shall dwell in the house of the Lord forever.

That is what we should desire and seek from the Good Shepherd – to dwell in the house of the Lord – forever.

THIRD SUNDAY AFTER EASTER

Readings: 1 Peter 2:11-19; John 16:16-22

Obedience to Lawful Authority

St. Peter wrote two letters that are included in the New Testament. Today our epistle reading is from his first letter which is one of the seven "Catholic Epistles": James, 1 & 2 Peter, 1, 2, 3 John and Jude. 1 Peter was written to the Christians in Asia Minor, the present day country of Turkey. In those days it was a Roman Province which eventually became Christian, before the Moslems conquered it.

At that time, in the 1st century, Christian converts lived in a hostile culture – that of Greek and Roman paganism. Christians were often ridiculed and persecuted in what we would now call a culture war. Peter calls them "strangers and pilgrims" because they are living in a hostile and foreign environment. He urges them to lead lives of virtue, lives of chastity and obedience to lawful authority. As such they are being called to give good example to pagans and also to members of their own family who are not Christian. The adults of the time were all converts and were baptized as adults; there were no cradle Catholics.

There was a problem of authority for Christians who were citizens of a pagan state. Should they obey Roman civil authorities or not? Peter says "Yes" because all authority comes from God. Jesus had stated that principle in his trial before Pilate (John 19:10-11) and St. Paul said the same thing in his Letter to the Romans (13:1-7). St. Peter says in today's reading that "by doing well you may put to silence the ignorance of foolish men." So Christians should obey Roman authorities in matters regarding taxes and the natural law.

Christians are free men who are not bound by the ceremonial laws of the Old Testament, but their freedom is not for license and sin. They are free to do what they should do.

They are free to respect others, to love the brothers, to fear God and to honor the king or civil authority. In this context he also urges slaves to obey their masters, since slavery at the time was an accepted part of civil society.

All legitimate authority is from God. The thinking of St. Peter here is that God is the Creator and source of all things, including authority in society and the Church. Authority in Church, State and family comes from God and is good for man who is a social being. Therefore man should be obedient to lawful authority – for his own good and for the good of society. Jesus was obedient to his parents and to his heavenly Father and he saved us by his obedience. We are not considering here unjust laws, like those relating to abortion and assisted suicide, which must be opposed. When the Jewish authorities forbade the Apostles to preach the Gospel, Peter replied by refusing to obey. He said to the high priest, "We must obey God rather than any human authority" (Acts 5:29).

Modern culture tends to be anti-authority and to exaggerate the freedom of the individual. The media have been glorifying rebels and anti-authority figures since the 1960s – presenting in a positive light anti-heroes in books, films, TV programs, music, magazine and newspapers. This started with Luther in the 16th century, and was increased in the "Age of Reason" and the French Revolution. Many of us were educated in this mentality in the schools we attended. "Obedience" therefore is a negative word in our culture. The media love to portray the modern "autonomous man" who, like a little god, determines for himself what is good and evil, what is true and false.

In the Church many orders of nuns have done away with Superiors and have replaced them with presidents or coordinators. Those congregations are disappearing because they do not attract young vocations.

Obedience to God and lawful human authority is praised often in the Bible. Psalm 119, the longest of the 150 Psalms, is all about obedience to God's law. Disobedience to lawful authority is a sin. It was the sin of Adam and Eve that brought suffering and death into the world. In the Old Testament obedience to God is rewarded and disobedience is punished severely as we see clearly in the Book of Judges. The view presented in the Old Testament is that the heavens and nature obey God – only man does not.

Jesus was obedient to his parents, Mary and Joseph (Luke 2:41-51). He was obedient to death, even to death on the cross St. Paul says in Philippians 2:8, and because of that God highly exalted him. Because of Jesus' obedience to the Father he saved us and made us children of God and heirs of Heaven.

Our Christian faith is a form of obedience to God who reveals his will to us. The "obedience of faith" (see Romans 1 & 16) leads to life with Christ and true freedom. Disobedience is a sin and leads to separation from God and death.

Conclusion

Obedience to lawful authority is a virtue, not a vice. In the First Book of Samuel we read that "obedience is better than sacrifice" (15:22). Everyone is subject to some authority: at home, at school, at work, while driving a car, in the Church, in civil society. God tells us in the Bible that proper obedience leads us to maturity and peaceful relations with others.

We have outstanding models of obedience in the Bible: Abraham, Moses, David, the prophets; in Mary who said "fiat" to the Angel Gabriel, in Joseph who obeyed the angel, in Jesus who in obedience died for us that he might save us. We can never thank him enough for that, for it is by his obedience that we have been justified and been made children of God and heirs of Heaven. We work out our salvation by being obedient to him.

True freedom comes from obedience to God, as Jesus says in John 8:31-32: "If you continue in my word, you are truly my disciples; and you will know the truth and the truth will make you free."

FOURTH SUNDAY AFTER EASTER

Readings: James 1:17-21; John 16:5-14

The Spirit of Truth

In today's Gospel Jesus tells his disciples that he will send them the Holy Spirit after he is gone from this world. The Holy Spirit is the third person of the Blessed Trinity. He proceeds from the Father and the Son and is co-equal to them in divinity. He is the Sanctifier who animates the Church, the body of Christ, just as the soul animates the human body. The Holy Spirit remains very mysterious for us, since it is hard for us to imagine him. He is a divine person but the primary visible images we have of him in the Bible are as a dove descending on Jesus, as wind, as tongues of fire upon the Apostles in the Upper Room on Pentecost Sunday.

Jesus calls him "The Spirit of Truth." He speaks the truth to the Church and reminds us of everything that Jesus told us during his earthly life. Jesus is the visible advocate of the Father, while the Holy Spirit is the "invisible" advocate. Since the Holy Spirit is the spirit of truth, it might be helpful to say something about the nature of truth.

Our culture is going through a crisis of truth. Simply put, if we ignore or reject truth, our civilization will collapse. Society cannot endure if truth is rejected and lies take its place, because freedom and harmony among men is based on truth (see John 8:31-32).

Truth is defined as the conformity of the mind to reality and is expressed in judgments, such as two plus two is four; every effect has a cause; whatever is, is; a thing cannot be and not be at the same time and in the same way (principle of non-contradiction). Truth is permanent, eternal – it does not change from day to day or year to year. What is true today cannot be false tomorrow.

Jesus said that the Holy Spirit is the spirit of truth. He is truth because he is God and God cannot lie or be false to himself. Jesus said of himself, "I am the way, the truth and the life" (John 14:6). In today's Gospel Jesus tells the Apostles that he will send them the Holy Spirit who "will teach you all the truth." This means that he makes his Catholic Church the depository of all truth necessary for salvation. The Father sends the Son to save us from our sins; the Son sends the Holy Spirit to teach us the truth and to sanctify us in truth and love.

Where do we find that truth? We find it in the Bible, in the liturgy of the Church, in the Creed, in the teaching of the Magisterium, and in the *Catechism of the Catholic Church.* Bishops in union with the Pope, assisted by their priests and deacons, have the duty and the authority to teach the truth to others.

Our culture has, to a great extent, adopted a philosophy of relativism. One might even say that this is the "Age of Relativism." Cardinal Joseph Ratzinger, before he was elected Pope Benedict XVI, spoke of the current "dictatorship of relativism" in western culture. This philosophy holds that there is no such thing as objective truth that transcends time and is permanent. It holds that what is true today can be false tomorrow; it holds that contradictory opinions, for example on the goodness or evil of abortion, can both be true. This false view of reality is implied in some popular sayings, such as "Have it your way," and "Create your own reality."

Many intellectuals, including some Catholics, deny that there is such a thing as absolute truth, for example, that lying is always wrong, that adultery is always wrong, that killing innocent persons is always wrong. Relativism is often defended by skeptics who claim that the human mind cannot attain any absolute truth, but then, illogically, they defend that proposition as absolutely true.

Often the basis of the defense of relativism is not reason, but morality. For, if there is no binding moral law that is always true and valid, especially no Ten Commandments, then everything is permitted, depending on the circumstances.

Dostoevsky said that if there is no God, all things are permitted. In more recent times this is called "situation ethics."

A good example of the exercise of relativism is found in the notion of "academic freedom" which is dominant in most of our universities and colleges. It is a nice sounding cover for total skepticism. Its defenders often deny the ability of the human mind to attain any truth. Again, it is defended as an absolute by professors who deny the existence of absolutes.

Such skepticism and relativism are reflected in our media every day. In many cases, the media are trying to manipulate public opinion rather than communicate the truth, for example, regarding abortion, homosexuality and embryonic stem cell research. Thus you will never see a graphic, hard-hitting presentation of an abortion on national TV.

The Holy Spirit, who is the spirit of truth, animates the Church. So the Catholic Church, and the Catholic Church alone, has the fullness of truth necessary for salvation. This was re-stated by the Holy See in the much-discussed document *Dominus Jesus* which was released in the year 2000.

The Holy Spirit is the "perfect gift" St. James mentions in today's Epistle. He says that "the Father of lights... has begotten us by the word of truth," that is, by the Gospel of Jesus Christ and his sacraments. Moreover, he also says that with God the Father "there is no change, or shadow of alteration," that is, truth does not change. Ideas have consequences, and the Gospel of Jesus Christ has eternal consequences. It does not change from day to day. If we believe in the Gospel and live by it, we are certain of attaining eternal life. There is nothing relative about that.

Conclusion

Let us thank God the Father, God the Son, and God the Holy Spirit for communicating their truth to the Church. Our task is to know it and to live it. We ask humbly for the grace to be faithful to the truth and to remain always in the truth. Our eternal salvation depends on it.

The last thought I will leave with you comes from St. James in today's Epistle: "Every good gift and every perfect gift is from above, coming down from the Father of lights, with whom there is no change, nor shadow of alteration." Amen.

FIFTH SUNDAY AFTER EASTER

Readings: James 1:22-27; John 16:23-30

Efficacious Prayer

Jesus is our model in the matter of prayer and today he tells us in the Gospel, "If you ask the Father anything in my name, he will give it to you." So the key to success in prayer is to pray in Jesus' name. Asking God for things we need is prayer, so our Lord is talking about efficacious prayer. If we want to obtain eternal life we must ask for it. Prayer therefore is absolutely necessary for salvation.

As we learned in our Catechism, prayer is raising our mind and heart to God; it is familiar conversation with God. A housewife complained to her pastor that she neglected to say her prayers. He asked her what the problem was. She replied, "Well, father, I spend so much time during the day talking to God that I don't have time to say my prayers." She was praying constantly, but did not realize it because she was not reading her prayer book.

There are various kinds of prayer. The first division is between liturgical prayer which is the prayer of the Church at Mass and in the Sacraments, and personal prayer. The latter is usually distinguished into vocal prayer and mental prayer. Vocal prayer is the Rosary and written prayers contained in a prayer book.

Mental prayer means thinking about God and engaging in familiar conversation with him. That is what the housewife was doing. There are various levels of mental prayer, such as meditation, contemplation, and transforming union with God.

In the liturgy of the Church we find four kinds of prayer: adoration, thanksgiving, petition and reparation. The Sacrifice of the Mass is primarily a prayer of adoration. The most common form of prayer is petition in which we ask God for our material and spiritual needs. Our petitions should always be in accordance with God's holy will, as Jesus prayed in Gethsemane "Not my will but thine be done."

The primary object of our prayer should be spiritual goods – the salvation of my soul and the grace to resist temptations and do the will of God. The secondary object is material and temporal things that contribute to our spiritual welfare.

The first characteristic of truly Christian prayer is that it be offered to God in the name of Jesus. So it is prayer made by one who is in the state of sanctifying grace or one who is in a state of sin and is asking God for the grace of conversion and change of heart. For, mortal sin destroys the living union with Christ which is the true basis of Christian prayer.

We should pray for an increase of faith, hope and charity. If other things are prayed for, they must be sought as helps to attain eternal life with God. Some pray to win the lottery and so become a millionaire, but winning the lottery may not be good for one's spiritual health and might result in losing one's soul. The lives of many winners of lotteries have been destroyed by the sudden acquisition of immense wealth. Since God alone knows what is best for us, readiness to accept his will is a fundamental condition of Christian prayer.

Some other dispositions of true Christian prayer are that one must pray: (1) with humility, recognizing our nothingness before God; (2) with perseverance, again and again and never giving up; (3) with sincerity and trust in God; (4) in solitude and silence so that one can concentrate on the presence of God.

Jesus Christ is our one Mediator with the Father (see 1

Timothy 2:5). Since he offers perfect worship to the Father, the Father listens to him and those united to him in his Body, the Church. God hears the sincere prayers of all, but especially of those whose life is in conformity with the Gospel of Jesus Christ. St. James tells us today that we must be doers of the word and not just hearers. He says therefore that our piety must be practical.

Our piety is practical when we control our tongue, which is difficult for most of us, and avoid speaking lies, calumny, detraction and gossip. We should help those in need, with both comforting words and helpful deeds. We should keep our heart free from the spirit of the world – from the concupiscence of the eyes, the concupiscence of the flesh, and the pride of life. This is very difficult in our secular world, especially for those who watch a lot of television, which is almost totally materialistic and this-worldly. Television is directed primarily to pleasure, wealth, physical health, pride and honors. Rarely, if ever, does it deal seriously with spiritual values, the existence of God, and eternal life after death.

Conclusion

In the prayers of the Mass the Church gives us the perfect example of what our prayers ought to be. Notice how sublime the petition is and how it is always made to God the Father, "Through Jesus Christ, Our Lord." We should be confident in our prayer because Jesus said, "If you ask the Father anything in my name, he will give it to you."

The Collect in today's Mass is an excellent prayer for all of us:

"O God, the source of all good, grant us your *inspiration* that we may have proper thoughts, and your *guidance* that we may carry them into practice. Through our Lord Jesus Christ, your Son, who lives and reigns with you in the unity of the Holy Spirit forever and ever. Amen."

That is prayer as recommended by our Lord and St. Paul.

ASCENSION OF OUR LORD

Readings: Acts 1:1-11; Mark 16:14-20

He Ascended into Heaven

Today we celebrate the great feast of the Ascension of Jesus into Heaven. We commemorate an event – briefly mentioned in the New Testament – that signifies Jesus' definitive departure in his physical presence from his budding Church. We learn from Luke that it took place on Mt. Olivet, opposite Jerusalem, 40 days after the Resurrection. The angels tell the disciples that this Jesus will not appear again on earth, except for the last judgment. However, we are not to think of him as separated from us, but rather as remaining with us invisibly by his grace as he goes to Heaven to prepare a place for us and to send forth his Spirit upon us before he returns to take us back forever with him (see John 14:3-4).

The Ascension of the Lord is the crowning event of the Resurrection and is intimately related to it. It is his official entry into the glory that was due him after the humiliation of Calvary; it is his return to the Father which he had foretold on Easter day: "I am ascending to my Father and your Father, to my God and your God" (John 20:17, in his words to Mary Magdalene).

And to the disciples on the way to Emmaus he had said: "Ought not the Christ to have suffered and so enter into his glory?" (Luke 24:26). This shows that he was not referring to a future glorification, but to one already present. Still, in order to strengthen his disciples in their faith, it was necessary for all of this to take place in a visible way over a certain period of time. For those who had seen our Lord die on the Cross, amid insults and jeers, must be witnesses of his final exaltation into Heaven.

This leads to the question: When did the Ascension take place? On Easter Sunday, as reported in Mark and Luke? Or 40 days later, as reported by Luke in Acts?

As you know, "40" is a round, perfect number for the

Hebrews, which means a certain length of time. For example, the Israelites wandered 40 years in the desert; Moses was on Mt. Sinai for 40 days; Jesus fasted for 40 days. It probably does not mean exactly 40 days, but a sufficient amount of time to get the job done. In general, the New Testament does not separate the Resurrection from the glorification of Jesus at the right hand of the Father. If Jesus delayed his Ascension literally 40 days, then his words to Magdalene (John 20:17) do not make much sense: "Go to my brethren and say to them, 'I am ascending to my Father and your Father, to my God and your God.'"

From the same Scriptures we know that Jesus associated in a familiar way with his disciples for some time; he instructed them; he met them in Galilee. So the physical seeing of him ascend into Heaven seems to indicate the end of his glorified physical presence in their midst. From now on they must live by faith and love and hope for his final coming in glory to judge the living and the dead.

The Ascension means that Jesus has definitively "entered into his glory" (Luke 24:26). His power and glory are supreme: "All authority in Heaven and on earth has been given to me," he says in Matthew 28:18, for as Mark adds, "the Lord Jesus was taken into Heaven and took his seat at God's right hand" (Mark 16:19).

Jesus' divine majesty and glory shine through his final words to his disciples. He speaks as one who can do everything when he predicts to his disciples that in his name "they will cast out demons.... They will lay their hands on the sick and they will recover" (Mark 16:17-18). The Acts of the Apostles bear witness to the truth of all of this.

Luke, both in his Gospel and in Acts, speaks of the great promise of the Holy Spirit who is to confirm the Apostles in their mission and in the powers they have received from Christ: "Behold, I send the promise of my Father upon you" (Luke 24:49); "You shall receive power when the Holy Spirit has come upon you; and you shall be my witnesses... to the end of the earth" (Acts 1:8).

As Christians, we are called to share in the entire mystery of Christ, and therefore also in his glorification. We share in it now by grace. Jesus said this himself: "I go to prepare a place for you, and when I go... I will come again and will take you to myself, that where I am, you may be also" (John 14:2-3). This indicates his victory over death and our share in it – if we are faithful.

The Ascension is therefore a strong support for hope for us who feel ourselves exiles in our pilgrimage through life, and suffer from being far from God. Where Jesus is, there we also shall be one day, if we are faithful to him. The foundation of our hope is his almighty power and his victory over death and sin and Satan.

Since he is our Head, and we are members of his body, we are already with him spiritually, as Augustine says in the second reading in the Liturgy of the Hours for Ascension Thursday.

Since Jesus no longer belongs to this present world of sin and death, but belongs in his whole being to the future and everlasting world of holiness and life, he cannot be detained on this earth or by it. The same will be true of us when we share in his glory through our persevering faith, hope and love.

The Lord is gone but he is not gone. He is gone in his visible presence to his Church, but he is always present to us by his Holy Spirit and his grace. "Behold, I am with you all days, even to the end of the world."

Another thought about the Ascension concerns the presence of Jesus' human nature in Heaven. What and where Heaven is remains a mystery to us, but Jesus is there with his glorified body – and so is Mary. He has taken our human nature with him into eternity. This is a mind-boggling idea, and we know that where he is we also shall be one day. As St. Paul says, he is "the pledge of our future glory" (Ephesians 1:14).

The Ascension is also closely connected with the sending of the Apostles into the whole world to witness to Christ and proclaim the Good News of salvation. Immediately after Jesus' Ascension, as the Apostles were still gazing into the sky, the angels told them to busy themselves with good works while they waited for the final coming of Christ. Christ's earthly mission in the flesh ends with the Ascension, and that of his disciples begins.

The Lord said to them: "Go therefore and make disciples of all nations, baptizing them in the name of the Father and of the Son and of the Holy Spirit" (Matthew 28:19). It was their duty, and that of the Church, to make his work of salvation permanent in the world by preaching, administering the Sacraments, and teaching men to live according to the Gospel.

Also, Jesus wanted them to prepare themselves by a period of prayer while they waited for the Holy Spirit who would confirm and strengthen them. Thus, the life of the Church began, not with action, but with prayer, together "with Mary, the Mother of Jesus" (Acts 1:14).

Let us join our prayer to that of Mary and the disciples in the Upper Room as we commemorate that first Novena, waiting for the sending of the Holy Spirit on Pentecost Sunday. We wait in hope and joy as we reflect that: "Christ has died, Christ is risen, Christ will come again."

SUNDAY AFTER THE ASCENSION

Readings: 1 Peter 4:7-11; John 15:26-27; 16:1-4

Witnesses for Christ

The nine days from Ascension Thursday to Pentecost Sunday are often called "the Novena of the Holy Spirit," in fact, the very first Christian novena. During this time the Apostles, with Mary the Mother of the Lord and the other disciples, remained in the Upper Room praying and waiting for the coming of the Holy Spirit. In his words before his passion Jesus instructed his Apostles about the Holy Spirit and his mission on earth to guide the Church in truth and holiness.

The Holy Spirit is the Third Person of the Blessed Trinity. In the Creed we profess that he is "the Lord and giver of life" and that he "proceeds from the Father and the Son; who together with the Father and the Son is adored and glorified." So the Holy Spirit is co-equal to the Father and the Son – there are three persons in one God. He is called in the New Testament "the Spirit of truth," "the Spirit of the Father and the Son," and also "the Spirit of Jesus" because Jesus sends him on the Church. He is our heavenly Advocate, the Gift of God, and the Promise of the Father. During Mass, the final three "*Kyrie Eleisons*" are directed to the Holy Spirit.

In the Gospel Reading today Jesus says that the Holy Spirit "will bear witness to me." So the Holy Spirit is a witness in the world to Christ. He is a witness to the divinity of Christ. At Jesus' baptism in the Jordan River the Father said loudly, "This is my beloved Son in whom I am well pleased," and immediately the Holy Spirit descended on him in the form of a dove and led him into the wilderness where he would fast and pray for forty days. On Pentecost Jesus sent the Holy Spirit on the Apostles to enlighten them about divine revelation and to strengthen them in enduring persecution for the sake of the Gospel.

The Holy Spirit is a witness to Jesus' mission as Messiah and Redeemer. He does this exteriorly by miracles and the gift of tongues at Pentecost. He does it interiorly by the infusion of divine grace on those who believe, leading to a life of virtue, prayer, charity and hospitality, as St. Peter mentions in today's Epistle.

The Holy Spirit is a witness to the teaching of Jesus. He, the Spirit of truth, will teach them all truth and remind them of everything Jesus said and did. He protects the Church in all her teaching and watches over her like a Guardian. He was with the Church in the beginning, and he is with the Church now.

The Holy Spirit transformed the Apostles into witnesses for Christ by their preaching with power and miracles. They told others what they saw and heard from Jesus and eventually converted the Roman Empire. They performed miracles in the name of Jesus. They witnessed by their suffering and death for the name of Jesus as he had predicted (John 16:1-4).

As faithful Christians we must also be witnesses to Christ by our words and deeds. We witness to him by professing our faith openly, by defending the Church against attacks from her enemies, by communicating the truth of Christ to others in any way we can. In our secular and now anti-Christian culture we must be counter-cultural by condemning and showing the errors involved in contraception, abortion, homosexuality, same sex marriage, and assisted suicide.

We witness to Christ also by our good example: by obeying Christ and his Church, by treating others justly, by being patient in suffering, and by striving to do God's will in all things.

Conclusion

We are not alone in our efforts to witness to Christ. He sends us his Holy Spirit to be our comforter, with his seven gifts, in times of trial and times of joy. We should pray to the Holy Spirit for light to know the truth, and for the strength to always do what is right, no matter what the obstacles may be. St. Paul says that we should "do the truth in charity" (Ephesians 4:15).

At the Last Supper Jesus warned his Apostles "If the world hates you, know that it hated me before you. If you were of the world, the world would love its own; but because you are not of the world, but I chose you out of the world, therefore the world hates you.... If they persecuted me, they will persecute you also" (John 15:18-20).

In this regard, in *The Imitation of Christ* we find the following prayer: "Grant, O Lord, that I may know what I ought to know; that I may love what I ought to love; that I may praise that which is most pleasing to thee; that I may esteem that which is valuable in thy sight; that I may despise that which is despicable in thy eyes" (Book III, 50).

In short, we pray for the grace from the Holy Spirit to reject whatever is evil and opposed to God, and to love and embrace all that is good and pleasing to God. This is the witness that Christ expects of us, his followers, in both word and deed.

PENTECOST SUNDAY

Readings: Acts 2:1-11; John 14:23-31

Lord and Giver of Life

Pentecost is the feast of the Holy Spirit which occurs fifty days after Easter. On this day we commemorate the sending of the Holy Spirit on the Church, and today on us, by the risen and glorified Christ who is seated at the right hand of God, the Father. Today we celebrate the visible coming of the Holy Spirit on the Church – manifested by a strong wind in the Upper Room where the disciples are gathered – and tongues "as of fire" descending on each one. The coming of the Holy Spirit signifies the maturity and sending forth of the Church to preach Christ to the whole world.

Pope Pius XII in his encyclical letter on the Mystical Body of Christ said that the Holy Spirit is "the soul of the Church" since he gives it light, life and strength. The word "spirit" itself means "breath" which is a sign of life. So the

Holy Spirit is the source of divine life in the Church and in each individual believer. He is called "holy" because he is God, the Third Person of the Blessed Trinity.

In the Creed at Sunday Mass we profess that the Holy Spirit is "the Lord and Giver of life." "Lord" signifies that he is God – the "*Kyrios*" of the Old Testament. "Giver of life" means that he is the cause of the spiritual life of our soul by grace. Since he proceeds from the Father and the Son and is of the same nature as they, he is co-equal in being and majesty with the Father and the Son. He manifested himself in the life of Jesus – at his conception in the womb of the Blessed Virgin Mary, at his Baptism in the Jordan River by John the Baptist, and in his public life.

Jesus sends the Holy Spirit on us as our Advocate, our Consoler, and Spirit of truth and love to instruct us and to help us to keep the commandments and to become holy persons.

The Holy Spirit has a special mission in the Church and in each individual. He spoke through the prophets in both the Old Testament and the New Testament. The Spirit therefore is the source or cause of divine prophecy and speaking in the name of God. In the New Testament Jesus came as the spirit-filled prophet and Messiah. The Gospels, and especially Matthew, portray Jesus as the fulfillment of all the prophecies of the Old Testament.

As "the soul of the Church" the Holy Spirit is the presence of God in his Church. His role is to teach the truth about God, man and the world and to sanctify the members of the Church. He is the love and life of God. He is our inspiration as the principle of love. As "the Spirit of truth" he is a teacher who reminds us of all that Jesus said and did (John 16). His activity in the Church is primarily interior, invisible, and mysterious in the souls of the faithful. By his grace he transforms us into images of Christ.

By his grace the Holy Spirit gives us an increase of faith, hope and charity which are directed to God and eternal life.

All Christians in the state of grace possess the Spirit (see John 14:23). There is no limit to our growth in knowledge and love of God. We pray today in the liturgy to be "filled" with the Holy Spirit. In addition to his grace, he gives us his seven gifts to help us grow in knowledge and love of God: wisdom, understanding, knowledge, counsel, fortitude, piety and fear of the Lord.

Conclusion

St. Luke says in the book of Acts that "they were all filled with the Holy Spirit and spoke in foreign tongues" (2:4). Pentecost is the fulfillment of Jesus' promise to his disciples, "If I go, I will send him to you" (John 16:7). It is the baptism he announced when he said "You will be baptized with the Holy Spirit" (Acts 1:5).

On the evening of Easter Sunday, the day of Jesus' resurrection from the dead, the gift of the Holy Spirit in the Upper Room was given to the disciples gathered there. Now, fifty days later, the sending of the Holy Spirit is for the whole Church – it is intended for everyone. Fundamental to the mission of the Holy Spirit is to bring about unity among human beings because he is the Spirit of love and love produces unity.

The Acts of the Apostles says that all heard Peter in their own language. The Church speaks all languages to all people on the face of the earth because she is meant for all.

St. Paul says in 1 Corinthians 12:13, "By one Spirit we were all baptized into one body." So the Spirit of love is the bond of union between believers – producing one body and one Church. So a person who causes division in the Church is not guided by the Holy Spirit – he is guided by some other spirit. The language of love, which is the language of the Holy Spirit, is understood by everyone. For this reason, we always need the renewal of Pentecost in order to grow in love of God and neighbor.

Even though we possess the Spirit, we should desire to receive him more fully. Just as we can always grow in knowledge, we can also always grow and increase in love. There is no limit. So we pray today with the liturgy of the Church: "Come, Holy spirit, fill the hearts of your faithful, and enkindle in them the fire of your love." Amen.

TRINITY SUNDAY

Readings: Romans 11:33-36; Matthew 28:18-20

Three and One

Our Mass today is in honor of the Holy Trinity, the most basic mystery of our Christian faith. The word "trinity" was coined in the 3rd century to express our belief that there are three persons in one God (trinity = three in one; Latin = *tres* + *unus*). The Trinity was not explicitly revealed in the Old Testament; Jesus revealed it in the New Testament when he spoke about the Father, the Son and the Holy Spirit. It is a matter of both oneness and threeness in God. According to our Catholic faith, God is one in nature. There is only one God, but there are three persons all sharing in the same divinity. In his preaching St. Patrick in Ireland used a shamrock to illustrate this truth – one leaf with three protrusions.

We profess faith in the Trinity when we make the Sign of the Cross – in the name of the Father and of the Son and of the Holy Spirit. We are baptized in the name of the same three persons and it is used often in the liturgy of the Church.

God therefore is both one and three, but not in the same respect. There is only one God – one essence, one substance, one nature. God is absolutely simple having no parts. He is uncreated, eternal and infinite in power. But at the same time there is a threeness in God, namely, three persons. Father, Son and Holy Spirit are not just three different names for the same reality, like my father who is also called George and dad. They are three distinct persons, but not separate because they are one in nature.

The first person in the Trinity is God the Father who is the source of all reality. He is the originator of all – the Creator of Heaven and earth. Jesus often prays to and refers to God the Father. He prays to him as "my Father," but he tells us to pray to him as "our Father." The reason for this is that Jesus is the natural son of the Father, while we are his adopted children. As such, we are also brothers of the Son and temples of the Holy Spirit.

The Son and the Holy Spirit are distinct persons and divine – equal in majesty to the Father. The Son is the Word with God (John 1). He was sent into the world to teach us the truth about God and the world. The distinctness and equality of the Persons is revealed by Jesus in the baptismal formula at the end of Matthew's Gospel: "Baptize them in the name of the Father, and of the Son, and of the Holy Spirit" (28:20).

The Holy Spirit is distinct from the Father and the Son and is also God. He was sent into the world by the Father and the Son to make us holy. In the Creed we say that he is "the Lord and Giver of life."

So there are three divine Persons in God but only one God. And God is absolutely simple, meaning there is no composition in God. That is part of the mystery. In God there is one intellect and one will, and the three Persons all share in the same divine nature through which they create and operate. Thus, where the Father is and acts, so do the Son and the Holy Spirit.

Catholic theology explains the three Persons as three substantial relations. These three relations in God are the Father as the origin and generator; the Son as generated by the Father, and also called the Word or Image of God; the Holy Spirit is spirated or breathed forth by the Father and the Son – he is the Gift of love. There is no priority of time between the three persons, since they are all eternal.

Each of the three Persons is in the others – there is a total mutual permeation. Thus Jesus said, "I am in the Father and the Father is in me" (John 14:10). Again, "I and the Father are one" (John 10:30). Again, "Philip, he who sees me has seen the Father" (John 14:9).

All activities of God outside of the inner life of God, like creation, are common to the three Persons. But we attribute creation to the Father, redemption to the Son, and sanctification to the Holy Spirit.

It is important to make a distinction between the Trinity it itself, in its inner life, and its external works of creation and sanctification. My relationship to the Trinity and my love of the Trinity are more important than theological knowledge about it. Some basic knowledge is necessary, but love is more important. Prayer and works of charity lead a person to the experience of the Trinity, that is, living the Christian faith and praying to all three Persons. Jesus said, "If anyone loves me, he will keep my commandments, and my Father will love him and we will come to him and make our home with him" (John 14:23). Here Jesus reveals to us the mystery of the divine indwelling in the soul of the believer. So we possess the Trinity within us when we are in the state of sanctifying grace.

Conclusion

The Holy Trinity is an absolute mystery – it is the mystery of mysteries which we will never comprehend. It is the most basic mystery of our Christian faith. A mystery is something hidden, veiled, unknown, and perhaps unknowable. We accept it in faith because Jesus revealed it and his infallible Church teaches it. We read in Hebrews 11:1, "Faith is the assurance of things hoped for, the conviction of things not seen."

The mystery of the Trinity is beyond reason, but not contrary to reason. The author of *The Cloud of Unknowing* put it this way: "By love God may be caught and held, by thinking never." Let us strive then to love and serve the Holy Trinity, in whose name we were baptized and made a Christian, as we try to return love for love. Today we should pray: "Glory be to the Father, and to the Son, and to the Holy Spirit: to the God who is, who was, and who is to come. Amen."

CORPUS CHRISTI

[Thursday after Trinity Sunday]

Readings: 1 Corinthians 11:23-29; John 6:56-59

Living Bread

This is the week of Corpus Christi which means "the Body of Christ." Today we will reflect briefly on this great mystery of faith. Since the 13th century Corpus Christi has been a major feast of the Church, usually with a solemn high Mass and a procession through the streets. If you read through your missal carefully you will note how often bread, food, and eating are mentioned in today's Mass.

Jesus refers to himself as "the Bread of life." All living things seek to preserve their life, for to them to live is to exist. Man needs food in order to live. The word "bread," as used by Jesus, can mean all food in general. We have an example of this in the "Our Father" when we say, "Give us this day our daily bread." Food is necessary to sustain the life of the body, but man also has a soul and a spiritual life. As Catholics we know that the life of the soul is given to us by God through faith and Baptism. In order to sustain that life we need God's grace, which is the life of the soul, through prayer and the Sacraments which are visible signs of invisible grace. The Mass and the Holy Eucharist are the main channels of grace or divine life for us.

The Body and Blood of Christ, given to us at Mass, are

the food and drink of the soul. Jesus said, "My flesh is food indeed and my blood is drink indeed" (John 6:56). This is "The Mystery of Faith." Through the words of the priest, Jesus changes bread to his Body and wine to his Blood. Both the humanity and the divinity of Jesus Christ are hidden under the humble appearances of bread and wine.

The Mass, as you know, is an unbloody re-presentation of the bloody sacrifice Jesus offered of himself to the Father on Calvary 2000 years ago. He offered himself to the Father for our sins and our eternal salvation. His motive is love for the Father and for us, so the Eucharist is also a mystery of love. A consequence of the sacrifice is the Real Presence of Jesus under the appearances of bread and wine. In the Mass he offers himself to us as food for our souls, because he is the bread of life.

Jesus said "He who eats my flesh and drinks my blood, abides (or remains or lives) in me, and I in him" (John 6:57). To abide or remain in him means to live in him and because of him through supernatural faith, hope and charity. This makes us children of God and heirs of Heaven.

All life comes from God who is infinite life, so to abide in him means to live, as he says, "As the living Father has sent me, and as I live because of the Father, so he who eats me shall also live because of me."

This is the living or "life-giving" bread from Heaven which surpasses the manna in the desert in the Old Testament which was a sign pointing to the Eucharist. "He who eats my flesh and drinks my blood has eternal life, and I will raise him up on the last day."

The Holy Eucharist is, therefore, God with us or Emmanuel. One of the themes of the Bible is that God wishes to be with his people. For example: with Adam and Eve, with Abraham, with Moses, with David, with Isaiah and the other prophets. He was with the Apostles and now he is with us in the Blessed Sacrament: "Behold, I am with you always even to the end of the world" (Matthew 28:20).

Conclusion

Today on the feast of Corpus Christi let us renew our faith in the Real Presence of Jesus in the Blessed Sacrament, which is the mystery of faith. It is also a mystery of love and hope for eternal life from God. We should thank Jesus for this wonderful miracle and strive to receive him in the Eucharist as often and as reverently as we can. St. Paul urges us to receive him worthily, that is, with a clean conscience in the state of grace. No one should receive Holy Communion when in the state of mortal sin – that just adds another mortal sin, the sin of sacrilege. A person who is guilty of this sin should go to confession as soon as possible.

We all want to live, and Jesus says to each one of us: "I am the living bread from Heaven, if anyone eats this bread he will live forever" (John 6:51-52). By receiving Holy Communion worthily, often and fervently we increase in sanctifying grace and so even now, in this life, already possess eternal life in a beginning way. This is our most precious gift from God.

SECOND SUNDAY AFTER PENTECOST

Readings: 1 John 3:13-18; Luke 14:16-24

A Great Supper

Today's Gospel reading presents a parable about a rich man giving a great banquet for his friends. Those invited refuse to come, so he invites the poor, the crippled, the blind and the lame. They enter the banquet hall but there is still plenty of room, so he invites everyone who wants to come in.

This is a parable which has a hidden meaning. The basic meaning of all Scripture is the literal interpretation. Everything else is based on that. On a deeper level there is what is known as the "spiritual" meaning of the Bible.

There are a further three levels of the spiritual meaning: (1) typology; (2) moral; (3) eschatological or pertaining to the four last things. Everything in the Old Testament points to Christ and the New Testament. St. Augustine said that the New Testament is hidden in the Old Testament, and that the Old is made manifest in the New.

Various texts point to Moses as a type of Christ. That is what is meant by typology. Often there is a moral aspect to a text. There is also a reference to the last things – death, judgment Heaven and hell, this is called the eschatological level of meaning.

The parable of the Great Supper can be understood in a spiritual sense as the Church. The man who invites his friends to the supper is a type of Christ who invites all to enter his Church. He first invites the Jews, and the leaders reject him. So his invitation goes out to all men to come to the Church – especially to the Eucharistic banquet. That banquet is the seven sacraments which offer grace and salvation to all. In this regard, St. Paul says in 1 Timothy 2:4 that God desires the salvation of all men and that all come to the knowledge of the truth.

The conditions of membership in his Church are faith and baptism. Faith means giving assent to the Creed, keeping the Ten Commandments, and practicing love of God and neighbor. One must believe in the Trinity and the Incarnation of God in Jesus of Nazareth. Whoever does that will be saved, provided that he keeps the Commandments and does the will of God.

This invitation has been given to each one of us. It is up to us to respond, not in word only but in deed and truth. Who invites us to the Eucharistic banquet? It is Jesus himself who said, "He who eats my flesh and drinks my blood has eternal life and I will raise him up on the last day."

What is the correct attitude of those invited? They should accept his invitation with eager faith and love. For example, Catholics who do not attend Mass on Sunday and rarely or never receive Holy Communion – at least worthily in the state of grace, are in danger of being shut out from the kingdom of God.

What are the penalties of those who reject the invitation? Jesus tells us that those who refused his invitation will never taste his supper. The invitation will not always be repeated: "If you do not eat the flesh of the Son of Man and drink his blood, you will not have life in you."

St. Ignatius Loyola in his famous *Spiritual Exercises* says that love is shown in deeds rather than in words. Words are cheap, but deeds are dear.

St. Ignatius may have gotten his idea from our epistle today by St. John: "My dear children, let us not love in word, neither with the tongue, but indeed and in truth" (1 John 3:18). The main task for us is to put our faith – what we believe – into action in our daily life. Pope Benedict XVI has said on several occasions that a major problem in the Church today is the lack of correspondence between faith and life.

Conclusion

Let us listen carefully to St. John today and heed his advice to us: "My dear children, let us not love in word, neither with the tongue, but in deed and in truth."

THIRD SUNDAY AFTER PENTECOST

Readings: 1 Peter 5:6-11; Luke 15:1-10

God's Merciful Love

Today's Gospel reading is about God's mercy – his merciful love. Mercy is a major theme in the Bible, especially in the Psalms and the four Gospels. In Ephesians 2:4 St. Paul tells us that God is "rich in mercy." Pope John Paul II, early in his pontificate, wrote a whole encyclical letter on mercy. Since

God is merciful and forgiving, as followers of Christ we are also called to be merciful in our dealings with others, and to have confidence in the merciful love of Jesus regarding ourselves.

You may ask, "What is mercy?" Mercy means coming to the aid of another in his need. It goes beyond compassion which means feeling sorry for or with another; it goes beyond compassion because it moves one to come to the aid of others in their suffering. In the Church there are religious groups called Sisters of Mercy and Fathers of Mercy. They were founded to help others, either physically or spiritually. They are dedicated to perform the corporal and spiritual works of mercy. Some religious congregations do both, such as the Franciscans and Mother Teresa's Missionaries of Charity. Contemplative orders lead a life of prayer and penance as spiritual help for others. Examples of this would be contemplative Carmelites, Trappists and Carthusians.

Because of his merciful love for us (Hebrew = *hesed*), God the Father created us and sent his only Son to redeem us from our sins and he sent the Holy Spirit to sanctify us. Since God is infinite love, he is also infinite mercy. God is not the author of sin. The source of sin and evil is to be found in the mystery of the misuse of free will in both angels and men. Trees and animals cannot sin because they do not have free will. They always do what God made them to do.

The mercy of Jesus is manifest because he became man, suffered and died for us to save us from our sins – to save us from hell and to open the gates of Heaven for those who die in the grace of God. Jesus expresses this in several places in the Gospels: "I have come into the world to seek and to save what was lost." "I have not come to call the just but sinners." "The Son of Man has not come to destroy souls, but to save them." So Jesus is our Savior, our Redeemer and our hope. He revealed himself to Sr. Faustina under the aspect of divine mercy and taught her to pray often: "Jesus, I trust in you."

The two parables in today's Gospel reading about the

lost sheep and the lost coin teach us about God's love for the sinner, and his intense efforts to bring about his conversion. Each one of us, either now or at some time in our life, is that lost sheep and that lost coin. God does not immediately destroy sinners – he searches carefully for them. He pursues the sinner with his grace like the Hound of Heaven, so powerfully expressed in Francis Thompson's poem of that name:

> I fled Him, down the nights and down the days;
> I fled Him, down the arches of the years;
> I fled Him, down the labyrinthine ways of my own mind;
> and in the mist of tears I hid from Him,
> and under running laughter.

His purpose is to bring the sinner to repentance and conversion. No sin is so great that God cannot or will not forgive it, provided one is truly repentant. God is rich in mercy and his mercy is everlasting, as we read in Palm 25:10: "All the ways of the Lord are mercy and faithfulness."

Please note the joy of the shepherd on finding the lost sheep, and the joy of the woman on finding the lost coin – one tenth of her money. This signifies the joy of God at the return of the sinner. God created us for eternal happiness, not for eternal rejection and pain.

In the parables about the Lost Sheep and the Lost Coin Jesus is telling us something about the nature of God – he is love and mercy. St. John tells us that God is love in 1 John 4. This should give us confidence that our sins are forgiven, no matter how serious they might be, if we have repented of them and received the absolution of the priest. Such confidence helps us to grow in the virtue of hope and trust in God and his providence – a virtue very much needed today. An excellent prayer in this regard is the short one recommended by Sister Faustina, "Jesus, I trust in you."

One of the many signs of Jesus' mercy is the fruits of the Mass. In itself the Mass is infinite because the victim, Jesus, is God and the High Priest of God. But the efficacy of the Mass is finite or limited because man is limited. Theologians distinguish the "general fruit" of the Mass as the grace given to all the members of the Church. The "special fruit" of the Mass is given to those for whom the Mass is offered. The "personal fruit" of the Mass is the grace that comes to the priest who offers the Mass and to those of the faithful in attendance.

Conclusion

Today let us ask Jesus, when he comes to us in Holy Communion, to help us penetrate the secrets of his infinite, merciful love for us.

FOURTH SUNDAY AFTER PENTECOST

Readings: Romans 8:18-23; Luke 5:1-11

Fishers of Men

The Sea of Galilee looks like a huge blue egg, about fourteen miles long and six miles across. At the northern shore, where the events in today's Gospel reading took place, there is lots of grass and gentle hills that form a type of amphitheater, suitable for people to sit down and listen to Jesus as he preached to them from St. Peter's boat.

Today's Gospel tells us about the call or vocation of the first Apostles, Peter, Andrew, James and John, who were fishermen on the Sea of Galilee. Jesus' teaching was often followed by a miracle. That is the case here. The miraculous catch of fish was a revelation of the divinity of Christ. When he invites them to follow him, Peter and the others respond with alacrity and humility; they leave all to follow him. By reflecting on this event we may learn something about God's dealings with ourselves – his call to each one of us and our response to him. In some sense, we are all called to be "fishers of men," to bear testimony to others of our faith in Jesus Christ.

Peter's call took place in ordinary circumstances – in a fishing boat on the lake. After preaching from Peter's boat, Jesus told him to lower his net for a catch of fish. Peter then protested, since as a fisherman he knew it was hopeless at that time of day and near the shore to try to catch fish. But he had faith in Jesus and so he said, "At your word I will lower the net." Peter was obedient to the Lord and as a result made a huge catch of fish which he immediately recognized as miraculous. Frightened by the power of Jesus, and recognizing his divinity, he fell to his knees and said, "Depart from me, O Lord, for I am a sinful man."

We see in this event that, faced with God's presence, man becomes aware of his nothingness, and feels a deep need to humble himself. Kneeling, as Peter did, is appropriate for this. Not just Peter, but all of them were "amazed" at the miraculous catch of fish – a normal reaction to an experience of the majesty of God.

There is a second level of meaning in this dramatic event. By giving preference to Peter, he singles him out for a position of leadership in his Church. The boat symbolizes the Church and Jesus' presence in the boat symbolizes his presence in the Church, her teaching and especially the Eucharist. The large catch of fish symbolizes the many members of the Church.

The condition of fallen man, after Adam's original sin, is one of labor. "In the sweat of thy brow shalt thou eat bread" (Genesis 3:19; and, "Man is born to labor, and the bird to fly" (Job 5:7). It is sad to work much and to accomplish little or nothing, as the four men did during the previous night of fishing. Similar to this is the lot of those who go through life in the state of mortal sin – they accomplish nothing by their labor that is meritorious of eternal life. They work without Christ and his grace who said clearly in John 15:5, "Without me you can do nothing," that is nothing that has value for eternal life with God.

Who are those who work apart from Jesus and whose

labors are worthless for Heaven? First of all, they are the ones who live in mortal sin. Without sanctifying grace, there is no merit, no advancement in union with God who is our final end. St. Paul said, "If I speak with the tongues of men and angels, and have not charity, I am become as sounding brass and tinkling cymbal" (1 Corinthians 13:1-3). If we pity the farmer who works hard and gets a small crop, still more miserable is the man who labors much but accomplishes nothing for eternal life. The riches and honors of this world, which he may accumulate for himself, have no value for his relationship with God.

Secondly, a condition of meritorious work is that it be done with the intention of doing the will of God and pleasing our Creator. If our actions are done for some evil purpose, such as vanity or lust or greed, they are devoid of merit in the eyes of God. God has created man for himself – our purpose is to glorify God and find our happiness in that. He shows his love for, and rewards those who refer all things to him. In the present case, Peter was obedient and humble so the Lord rewarded him – and made him and his successors his vicar on earth.

Conclusion

If we have labored without Christ and without his grace, now is the time to change direction – now is the time to seek the will of God in all things.

Human life is a struggle, filled with suffering and disappointments. In this regard, St. Paul in today's Epistle says to you and to me that "the sufferings of the present time are not worthy to be compared with the glory to come that will be revealed in us… as we wait for the redemption of our body, in Christ Jesus our Lord" (Romans 8:18 & 23). These words should fill our hearts with hope and confidence that God will come to our assistance if we ask him with humility, and persevere in prayer and good works.

FIFTH SUNDAY AFTER PENTECOST

Readings: 1 Peter 3:8-15; Matthew 5:20-24

Anger: Just and Sinful

Anger is one of the seven capital sins. These sins are called "capital" because many other evils flow from them. The sin of anger can lead to cursing, blasphemy, physical injury, murder, violations of charity and justice. In the Gospel reading for today Jesus warns us against willful and sinful anger which God judges severely.

We know from experience that feelings of anger can rise up in us quickly when we are offended in some way or another. A virtuous man controls his feelings. If we give in to feelings of anger, we may injure others by word or deed and damage good relations with others. People who give in to anger, and utter harsh words or strike another, can lose a lifelong friend or alienate a close relative.

There are several examples of the consequences of giving in to anger. In a fit of anger, Cain killed his brother, Abel. King Saul persecuted David and tried to kill him on several occasions. Absalom, the son of David, killed his brother Amnon.

Anger is an outburst of emotion that is connected with the desire for revenge. St. Thomas Aquinas said that anger is "the impulse to avenge an injury which one has suffered." Often it leads to loud shouting, a flushed face, harsh words and the waving of one's arms. We read about it in the newspapers daily; we see it portrayed in films and television programs; we see it in professional sports on TV. Car accidents are often followed with angry words, gestures, shouting; it is what is now called "road rage."

As an inordinate outburst of emotion because of some offense, anger is a venial sin; but it could be a mortal sin if one flies into a rage, acts unreasonably, loses control of himself and attacks the offender. As an inordinate desire for revenge, anger is opposed to charity or justice and so could be a mortal sin. If the matter is trivial, it would be a venial sin.

There is, however, such a thing as a just anger, that is, anger which is a righteous indignation over sin and which involves an orderly desire for punishment, such as a father punishing a disobedient son.

We read in the New Testament that Jesus used a type of whip to drive the buyers and sellers out of the temple in Jerusalem. Moses was justly angry at his brother, Aaron and the people, for setting up a golden calf and worshiping it (Exodus 32). So there is such a thing as just anger, but it is difficult to control and avoid sin. Since anger is an emotion or feeling, it can arise immediately and without our willing it; we cannot do anything about that. Such a feeling is not a sin because it is not willed. But we can control the consequences of anger – by holding our tongue and not doing anything rash. We always remain free.

Man's actions should be under the control of reason. Anger clouds one's reason; it is a type of temporary insanity. We should never take a serious decision when we are angry, nor should one utter harsh words. If something must be said or done, it is best to wait until one is calm and not under the influence of anger.

So anger is a passion which blinds the mind and is difficult to control. If we give in to it, it is a sin and leads to many evils. That is why it is included in the seven capital sins. We read in the Old Testament: "Give up your anger, and forsake wrath; be not vexed, it will only harm you" (Psalm 37:8).

In the Epistle today St. Peter suggests remedies against anger: fraternal harmony and mutual charity. He urges us to love the brethren, to be merciful and humble, to be united in prayer and to be of one mind. He says, "Refrain your tongue from evil" and "If you suffer anything for the sake of justice, you are blessed."

As followers of Christ we should not "render evil for evil,

or abuse for abuse." The norm of "an eye for an eye" of the Old Testament was rejected by Jesus because it leads to a cycle of revenge. His new commandment is "turn the other cheek" as the way to stop a cycle of violence. We see this in the patience and meekness of the martyrs, especially in St. Maximilian Kolbe.

We should praise and imitate the Lord Jesus in our hearts. Like him, we should be "meek and humble of heart (Matthew 11:28). Like him, we should "seek after peace and pursue it" (Psalm 34).

Conclusion

If we have offended anyone by our anger, our Lord tells us not to try to offer anything to God until we are again on good terms with our neighbor. In fact, he urges us to take the initiative: "Go first to be reconciled to thy brother (i.e., neighbor), and then come to offer thy gift."

The judgment of God is a frightful thing: "It is a fearful thing to fall into the hands of the living God" (Hebrews 10:31). So remember the Lord's words: "Everyone who is angry with his brother shall be liable to judgment." According to the "Our Father," if we forgive others, the Father will forgive us. We say to the Father: "Forgive us our trespasses, *AS* we forgive those who trespass against us."

"Jesus meek and humble of heart, make our hearts like unto thine."

SIXTH SUNDAY AFTER PENTECOST

Readings: Romans 6:3-11; Mark 8:1-9

Born Again by Water

Today I want to call your attention to the Epistle of St. Paul in which he speaks about Baptism. I will remind you about some of the great truths connected with the Sacrament of Baptism. We are so familiar with Baptism – especially the Baptism of babies – that we may forget how important it is. First of all, Baptism is necessary for salvation as St. John tells us in 3:5. Baptism was prefigured in the Old Testament by the water associated with Noah's ark, the people of Israel crossing through the Red Sea, and the same people crossing over the Jordan River into the Promised Land.

Baptism is the foundation of the whole Christian life: it is the gateway to life in the Spirit; it is the door that gives us access to the other sacraments. Through Baptism we are freed from all sin – both original sin and our own personal sins. By Baptism we are reborn as children of God and so we become members of the Body of Christ, incorporated into his Church and made sharers in her mission. Along with sanctifying grace we also receive the infused theological virtues of faith, hope and charity; we receive the four moral, cardinal virtues of prudence, justice, temperance and fortitude and the seven gifts of the Holy Spirit.

Baptism is defined as "the sacrament of regeneration through water and the word" (see CCC #1213; Rom. Cat. II, 2, 5). Water is involved in our birth into this world of time and space; water is essential for Baptism which gives us eternal life. The word "baptize" is taken from the Greek word which means to plunge or immerse someone in water. It has to do with washing or cleansing as in a bath; in Baptism it signifies spiritual cleansing from sin.

The immersion into water also symbolizes burial into Christ's death; coming up out of the water symbolizes

Christ's resurrection from the dead. The result is that man becomes "a new creature." That is what St. Paul is describing in today's Epistle from Romans 6.

There are two main aspects to Baptism. The first is purification from all sin. St. Paul today calls this "baptism into his death." This means that the baptized person is cleansed of all sin, but concupiscence or an attraction to sin remains. The Church says that this concupiscence itself is not sin, but it can lead us to sin. The second aspect is regeneration into a new life, becoming a new creature. The infusion of grace produces an internal change in the newly baptized person. He now participates in the life of God; he is "reborn" to a new, spiritual life. He becomes a member of Christ's Body, the Church, a child of God and heir of Heaven. Where Christ now is in glory, we also shall be, if we remain faithful to him and avoid all mortal sins which are the death of the soul.

In order to persevere in grace and nourish our new life in Christ, we must follow him in suffering and in joy, in good times and in bad. Jesus promised, "Those who love me will keep my word, and my Father will love them, and we will come to them and make our home with them" (John 14:23). So we must avoid all sin and the near occasions of sin, such as immoral films, television and pornography on the Internet. In our debased, secular culture this means rejecting many things that are taken for granted by others – materialism, consumerism, immodesty in dress, and sexual permissiveness. To counter that, we must develop our spiritual life and union with God by personal prayer and regular reception of the Sacraments, especially the Holy Eucharist and Penance.

If we are not alert Catholics, we can easily adopt the ways of the world around us – perhaps unaware of what we are doing. These false attitudes permeate much of prime time TV, movies, modern music and the print media.

Baptism also imprints on us a character or indelible

mark of being children of God – nothing can erase it, not even heresy or apostasy. We are "Marked" for all eternity as members of Christ's Body. A similar character comes with Confirmation and Holy Orders and that is why they cannot be repeated – they can be received only once.

Conclusion

In order to be saved we must preserve the grace of Baptism at all cost. When St. Paul says we die and are buried with Christ, he means that we die to sin and reject all sin – we die in a spiritual sense. St. Paul said of himself "I die daily." To do this and to persevere, we must cling to Christ by receiving the Sacraments regularly and by personal prayer.

The person who truly prays with faith daily, and receives Holy Communion often, is dead to sin and alive to God in Christ Jesus our Lord. That is the type of Catholic St. Paul urges us to be in today's Epistle – a Christian just like him who imitates Jesus Christ.

SEVENTH SUNDAY AFTER PENTECOST

Readings: Romans 6:15-23; Matthew 7:15-21

Beware of False Prophets

In today's Gospel reading, taken from the Sermon on the Mount, our Lord warns us to "beware of false prophets." There were many false prophets in the Old Testament and in the time of Jesus, such as the leaders of the people like the Scribes and Pharisees. There are many false prophets today – both inside the Church and outside of the Church. We will consider what a prophet is and how to distinguish between true a true prophet and a false prophet.

A prophet is one who "speaks before others" or "for another." In the Bible the word usually refers to those individuals who are inspired by God to speak his word to the community. We see that realized in prophets like Samuel, Nathan, Amos, Isaiah, Jeremiah and John the Baptist, to mention just a few.

The message they give, the prophecy they utter is not their own – it is from God. Often the true prophet says, either before or after the prophecy, "Thus says the Lord." There are several signs of true prophets: (1) They are known by the integrity and holiness of their lives. They keep the Ten Commandments, they observe the Law, and they condemn all forms of idolatry; (2) when a true prophet foretells something, it happens; (3) true prophets are often persecuted for telling the truth, like Jeremiah. In a certain sense, true prophets are also "mystics," like Isaiah and Ezekiel, because of their close experience of God and their ecstatic visions.

A false prophet is one who claims to speak for God, but does not. He is a liar and deceiver. He gives his own messages, ideas and false prophecies, but claims he is speaking for God. They appear to speak the truth, but they contradict some teaching of the Church on either doctrine or morals. Some are easy to recognize, but others are very clever and hide their agenda under ambiguous language. Jesus tells us that we can recognize them from their fruits: "By their fruits you shall know them" (Matthew 7:16). Good trees produce good fruit; bad trees produce bad fruit – you know the tree from its fruits. Likewise, you know the false prophets from their deeds and their projects.

Our Lord says the false prophets appear in public wearing "sheep's clothing," that is, they appear outwardly to be Christians, to be friendly, to be truly Catholic, but "inwardly they are ravenous wolves." They have their own agenda which is not that of Christ; they hate the Church or some part of Church teaching; they appeal to man's base instincts. They often encourage pride, disobedience to legitimate authority, division and sensuality.

Jesus warns us to "Beware of false prophets." Be on

your guard against them! Who are they? How can I recognize them? False prophets are politically correct – they go along with the crowd and wish to please the world. They tell you to "do your own thing"; they tell you the Church is wrong in her teaching on sex – contraception, fornication, adultery, homosexuality, divorce and remarriage. They tell you the Church is wrong in her teaching on life: abortion, euthanasia, surrogate motherhood, in vitro fertilization and assisted suicide. They tell you the Church oppresses women and is "sexist," that she is wrong in not ordaining women to the priesthood.

In our present culture, who are the false prophets? Outside the Church, there are many of them in the media – television, radio, print media, music, and on the op-ed page of certain popular newspapers. Inside the Church they are dissenters and teachers of error. In a word, those who contradict the official teaching of the Holy Catholic Church are false prophets. Our divine Lord tells us, "Beware of them." By their fruits you will know them.

We should thank God every day that we have the Pope and the Magisterium of the Church to teach the true faith as given to us by Christ and the Apostles. The Magisterium of the Church protects us against the errors and deceptions of the false prophets.

Not all who claim to be Catholic are in fact Catholic. They are Catholic in name only, not in reality. In proof of this our Lord says, "Not everyone who says to me 'Lord, Lord,' will enter the Kingdom of Heaven, but only the one who does the will of my Father in Heaven." What is required is not words, but deeds – doing the will of the Father by keeping the commandments.

Conclusion

We should be true prophets by doing the will of the Father, by living according to the truths we profess to believe. As

St. Paul says in today's Epistle by our faith and Baptism we are free from sin and servants of God who is our source of eternal life. "For the wages of sin is death, but the gift of God is life everlasting in Christ Jesus our Lord."

As diligent and informed Catholics we should follow our Lord's advice to beware of false prophets. By their fruits you shall know them.

EIGHTH SUNDAY AFTER PENTECOST

Readings: Romans 8:12-17; Luke 16:1-9

The Rich Man and the Steward

Everything we have is a gift from God. This includes our body, our mind, our physical and spiritual talents, and whatever material goods we may possess. Since they were given to us by God, they come first from him. This means that we are not absolute masters, but that we are rather stewards of God's creation and should use things in the way in which God intended them to be used. The final purpose of our human existence, the reason why God created us is that we might attain Heaven, eternal life in the face-to-face vision of God.

A major source of source of evil in the world is the secular attitude that man is the sole owner of all he possesses, that he can do as he pleases with his possessions, that he is not accountable to anyone except himself. This is a false understanding of what man is and Jesus offers a correction in the Gospel reading for today.

The message from our culture is diametrically opposed to what Jesus says. The world says: There is no objective law one must conform to; there is no divine or natural law; man is autonomous – therefore "do your own thing"; gratify yourself, especially in food, drink and sex; accumulate as much wealth as you can, since wealth guarantees access to power, fame and sex; you are accountable to no one but yourself, so you can create your own reality; form your conscience according to your own ideas, even in opposition to the teaching of the Church.

The Gospel message of Jesus is very different. He says: Seek first the kingdom of God and all these things will be given to you; Blessed are the poor in spirit, for theirs is the Kingdom of Heaven; love God above all things and your neighbor as yourself; seek heavenly goods first, not earthly; seek the eternal first because they last, not the temporal which are passing away.

Jesus says that the Kingdom of Heaven is like a treasure hidden in a field; it is like a pearl of great price. Sacrifice everything to possess it. St. Augustine said on one occasion, "What is not eternal is nothing."

In today's parable, God is the "rich man" and we are his stewards, his agents, so we must use our talents wisely, according to God's law. Eventually, at the judgment we will have to give an accounting of our stewardship. Since God is bountiful and generous to us, we in turn should be generous in using our talents and goods to help others because we are social beings and reach maturity by developing good relations with others. We should not be selfish, but rather generous, like God, and share what we have with others in need.

We might be shocked at the praise the master heaps on the unjust steward. In reality, he is not praising his dishonesty. The master praises the unjust steward for his cunning and foresight, but not for his injustice. The point is that the children of this world are more prudent in providing for their future than are the children of light.

Conclusion

Through prayer, keeping the commandments and helping others in need we should be more diligent in loving God and serving our neighbor than the children of this world are in seeking wealth and pleasure. Their pleasures are temporal and do not last, and they will go to hell and perdition if they do not change their ways and repent. The prize we seek is permanent, lasting – it is eternal life with the Father, the Son and the Holy Spirit. We should make our own these words of our Savior: "Seek first the kingdom of God and his justice, and all these things will be given to you besides."

Let us listen to what St. Paul says about the difference between temporal and heavenly riches: "If then you have been raised with Christ, seek the things that are above, where Christ is seated at the right hand of God. Set your minds on things that are above, not on things that are on earth. For you have died (to sin) and your life is hidden with Christ in God" (Colossians 3:1-3).

Finally, we should consider this good advice in the very first chapter of *The Imitation of Christ*: "Vanity of vanities, and all is vanity, except to love God and serve Him alone.... This is the highest wisdom, by despising the world to tend to heavenly kingdoms.... Study therefore to withdraw thy heart from the love of visible things, and to turn thyself to things invisible. For they that follow their sensuality defile their conscience and lose the grace of God." God bless you.

NINTH SUNDAY AFTER PENTECOST

Readings: 1 Corinthians 10:6-13; Luke 19:41-47

Cooperation with God

The theme of today's Mass is correspondence with God's grace – cooperation with God for our sanctification and salvation. The opposite side of that is what happens to those who disobey God and go their own way. In the Epistle St. Paul gives four examples from the Old Testament, Exodus and

Numbers, of disobedience to God and the punishment for it. Likewise, in the Gospel Reading for today Jesus weeps over the city of Jerusalem because of what will happen to it in forty years under the Roman generals, Titus and Vespasian. He weeps over their obstinacy in sin and the suffering they will endure because of it. This will happen because Jerusalem rejected its Messiah and Savior, Jesus Christ, just as the Israelites in the wilderness were punished for rejecting God grace and falling into idolatry.

Grace is a supernatural favor – the free and undeserved help that God gives us to enable us to respond to his call to become children of God (CCC 1996). Grace is a free gift and undeserved because it is wholly supernatural. Grace transforms us and makes us become children of God, members of the Body of Christ and heirs of Heaven. Grace is a share, a participation in divine life. This is the "pearl of great price," "the treasure hidden in a field" that we considered last Sunday.

There are two basic kinds of grace which are called actual grace and sanctifying grace. Actual grace is a *temporary* help from God to overcome temptation, to practice virtue; it is given to unbelievers to help them to accept divine revelation and make an act of faith in Jesus Christ as the Son of God and their Savior. Sanctifying grace is a *habitual or permanent* quality of the soul which transforms the person into a new creature in a spiritual sense – he is now a child of God and partaker in the divine life.

We know from divine revelation that God's grace is offered to all persons, but in varying degrees according to God's providence. Thus, St. Paul says in 1 Timothy 2:4 that God "desires everyone to be saved and to come to the knowledge of the truth."

Because of our fallen nature which we have inherited from Adam, we are subject to temptation, that is, a certain enticement to sin and rebellion against God. There are many examples of that in the Bible – Adam and Eve, King Saul, King David, Peter and Judas. In his mercy, though, God does not allow us to be tempted beyond our power to resist. In support of this St. Paul says, "God is faithful and will not permit you to be tempted beyond your strength" (1 Corinthians 10:13).

Grace is not overpowering; it is not irresistible; it does not violate man's freedom, for God deals with man in accordance with the nature of his freedom of will. The Israelites in the Old Testament rejected God's grace and were punished – for idolatry, fornication and disobedience. Jerusalem rejected Jesus and was punished by total destruction – not a stone left on a stone. These events are warnings to us that if we reject God' grace, are disobedient, violate his commandments, we will be punished for it – even in this life, or worse, in the next life. The Bible is clear on this point: Those who disobey God and break his laws will be punished. But since God is infinite mercy, he punishes the sinner in this life in order to bring him to repentance. This truth is taught often in the book of Judges.

What we all need is perseverance in grace. To do that, we need humility and trust in God. St. Paul warns us today, "Let him who thinks he stands take heed lest he fall" (1 Corinthians 10:12). In order to persevere in grace for a long time, for the rest of our life to the moment of death, we need a special help or grace from God. Perseverance means fidelity to God in all things.

Perseverance in grace is acquired by constant prayer, self discipline and frequenting the sacraments, especially Holy Communion and regular Confession. One of the Fathers of the Church said that frequent Communion is "the medicine of immortality." The French theologian de la Taille called the Holy Eucharist "The Sacrament of Perseverance." St. Augustine said that final perseverance in grace, which is our ticket to Heaven, is a great gift from God.

Conclusion

We must be firmly convinced that we need the grace of God in order to persevere in virtue and to overcome all the temptations we are subject to. We should pray often and beg God for perseverance, especially the grace of final perseverance, which means that we die in the state of sanctifying grace. We need to pray for this insistently, as our Lord recommends: "Ask and you shall receive, seek and you shall find, knock and it will be opened to you" (Matthew 7:7).

May God grant each one of us the great gift of final perseverance – of overcoming all temptations and dying in the state of sanctifying grace. This is the treasure found in a field; this is the pearl of great price. Amen.

TENTH SUNDAY AFTER PENTECOST

Readings: 1 Corinthians 12:2-11; Luke 18:9-14

The Pharisee and the Publican

Jesus was an outstanding teacher who made abundant use of stories and parables to illustrate divine truth. The parable of the Pharisee and the Publican is one of his most memorable parables. It ranks with the Good Samaritan and the Prodigal Son. In this parable the divine teacher is warning us to avoid pride and to practice humility. He is also giving us an example of how to pray.

In the parable of the Pharisee and the Publican Jesus distinguishes two types of men: (1) those who trust in themselves, think themselves better than others, and despise others as inferior – the proud; (2) those who trust in God, are aware of their own weakness and sins, and look upon other as better than they are – the humble.

Pride is an inordinate esteem of oneself. It is contrary to the truth – it is a lie. The proud person attributes all good qualities to himself, minimizes or denies defects, and claims to possess qualities he does not have. The proud person does not recognize his dependence on God and refuses to submit to God. Pride like this is one of the seven capital sins.

St. Ignatius Loyola, in his famous *Spiritual Exercises*, says that the strategy of the devil in temptation is to tempt one to covet riches, which leads to honors in this world, which leads to pride. The proud person then falls into many sins. We see that often times in the lives of the rich and famous.

Humility is the moral virtue which keeps a person from reaching beyond himself. It enables us to restrain the inordinate desire of our own excellence. It moderates the desire for the esteem and approval of others. True humility is based on self-knowledge. It enables us to see ourselves as we really are in the eyes of God. The word humility comes from the Latin *humus* which means "ground" or "lowly."

St. Thomas Aquinas says we should recognize two things in ourselves: (1) what we have from God, and (2) what we have from ourselves. Our goodness and virtues come from God; our defects and imperfections come from ourselves because of the misuse of our will. Humility is a fundamental virtue of the spiritual life because it removes the obstacles to the reception of grace. St. James says explicitly that God resists the proud and gives his grace to the humble (4:6). This means that humility is necessary for salvation. God hears the prayers of the humble according to the wise man in the Old Testament, "The prayer of the humble pierces the clouds" (Sirach 35:17).

The Bible and the lives of the saints give us many examples of humility. Moses is described as the humblest of men. David was a sinner but, like the Publican in today's Gospel reading, he humbled himself before God and was forgiven his sins. The Blessed Virgin Mary humbled herself before God and said to the angel, "Behold the handmaid of the Lord. Let it be done unto me according to your word." St. John the Baptist said in reference to Jesus, "He must increase and I must decrease." St. Paul writes in Philippians 2 that Jesus humbled himself and became obedient unto death – even death on the cross. And Jesus said of himself, "Learn of me for I am meek and humble of heart" (Matthew 11:29). The saints considered others better than themselves because they contrasted their own sins and weaknesses with the virtues of others and the majesty of God.

What was the result of the prayer of the Pharisee and the Publican? Two different dispositions brought about two different results: (1) the Publican was forgiven his sins and he found grace with God; (2) the Pharisee returned home with one more sin on his soul. These are the effects of humility and pride. It is a fundamental principle of Christianity that humility will be rewarded with glory, and pride will punished with degradation.

Conclusion

Our Lord warns us today that "Everyone who exalts himself shall be humbled, and he who humbles himself shall be exalted" (Luke 18:14). We should attend Mass and offer our prayers with a deep spirit of humility and sorrow for our sins, like the sinner in today's parable.

Let us pray with the Publican: "O God, be merciful to me a sinner." His prayer had the qualities that our prayers should have – it was humble, contrite and confident. An excellent example of this is what is known as "The Jesus Prayer": "Lord Jesus Christ, Son of the living God, have mercy on me, a sinner."

During the day we should reflect on these solemn words of Jesus that apply to each one of us: "Everyone who exalts himself will be humbled, and he who humbles himself will be exalted." Jesus, Mary and Joseph are outstanding examples of humble persons who were exalted.

ELEVENTH SUNDAY AFTER PENTECOST

Readings: 1 Corinthians 15:1-10; Mark 7:31-37

Sacred Rites and Symbols

Jesus is presented often in the Gospels as a miracle worker. He cures physical illnesses and forgives sins as a sign of his divinity. Sometimes he works a miracle by words, sometimes he does it by a mere act of his will, and other times he uses actions. In today's Gospel Reading he cures a deaf and dumb man through the use of symbolic actions – a type of ritual, probably to arouse faith in the afflicted man. The Church uses symbolic actions or rituals in the administration of her sacraments, especially Baptism and Holy Eucharist, which are visible signs of invisible grace.

Fr. John Hardon says in his *Modern Catholic Dictionary* that ritual is "the prescribed words and ceremonies for a religious service; also all the sacred rites in use in the Church." Symbols and ritual are natural to man because he is a symbol-making being as we see in the case of language, works of art, computer icons, and logos used by companies to identify themselves.

We heard today in the reading of the Gospel that Jesus was asked to lay his hands on a man who could not hear or speak. "Laying on of hands" signifies a transfer of power. In the Church we have an example of this in the Sacrament of Holy Orders when the bishop ordains a new priest by laying his hands on the head of the candidate. Here Jesus uses his fingers to touch the man's ears and tongue. The fingers are also a symbol of power. In the *Veni Creator Spiritus* the Church invokes "the finger of the right hand of God" to come to our aid.

All know that saliva has a soothing effect on minor cuts and burns and we usually bring a finger to the mouth when it has been injured. Jesus uses the symbolism of his fingers before he cures the man by an act of his will. He could have done it by a mere word or thought, but he used a sign.

Since man is composed of body and soul, symbols are very important, that is, visible signs to signify invisible thoughts and desires. Man loves ritual and this love is made manifest in birthdays, weddings, anniversaries, funerals, the Fourth of July, the inauguration of a president, etc.

Our sacraments are surrounded with ritual and the rites should not be changed without good reason and explanation. Baptism, Eucharist, Matrimony and the Anointing of the Sick are sacraments and sacred signs of invisible grace. One of the main reasons for the present confusion in the Church is the wholesale abandonment of many traditional rites that identified a Catholic – changes in the Mass, dropping Friday abstinence from meat, fasting during Lent, the Rosary, and evening devotions in church such as novenas.

Major changes in the Church were introduced after Vatican II quickly and without proper explanation. Some priests changed the rites on their own authority – contrary to Church law. Many of these changes were actually contrary to what Vatican II had said, but the claim was made that the changes were in "the spirit of Vatican II."

By his actions and will Jesus opened the ears and unloosed the tongue of the handicapped man. He performed the miracle with signs. Something similar takes place in Baptism when the child or adult is washed with water and the Holy Trinity is invoked. The effect of Baptism is that sanctifying grace is infused into the soul so that we become dead to sin and alive to God. Baptism opens our ears to hear and our heart to accept the word of God. It empowers our tongue and lips to proclaim God's mighty deeds – to praise him, to thank him for his many gifts, and to ask him for favors.

Before being baptized we were deaf and dumb spiritually. Jesus has given us light and life through his divine grace. The New Testament says that "He made the deaf to hear and the dumb to speak" – and that applies to us also through our reception of Baptism.

Like St. Paul, it is our duty to proclaim the Good News by the example of our lives as Christians and by our words. What is the Good News or the Gospel? It is that God became man in Jesus Christ, that he died for us according to the Scriptures, that he rose again on the third day according to the Scriptures, that he ascended into Heaven where he intercedes for us with the Father. That is the Good News which gives rise to faith, hope and charity by which we are saved. The Apostles preached it and died for it – so did St. Paul and all the saints. It is communicated to us by the sacraments which are sacred rites. We should love and treasure the rites of the Church and her sacraments.

Conclusion

Let us pray today to be faithful to the grace given to us in Baptism and the other sacraments. So we can say truthfully with St. Paul, "By the grace of God I am what I am, and his grace in me has not been fruitless."

TWELFTH SUNDAY AFTER PENTECOST

Readings: 2 Corinthians 3:4-9; Luke 10:23-37

Who Is My Neighbor?

In the opening two verses of today's Gospel reading Jesus tells his disciples that he is the fulfillment of all the promises to Israel recorded in the Scriptures. Prophets like Jeremiah and kings like David desired to see the Messiah, but did not see him. We, like those disciples, are blessed because we see the fulfillment of all the prophecies in Jesus.

One lawyer in the audience stood up and asked him a question as a type of test: "What must I do to attain eternal life?" This is an excellent question; it is a fundamental question for all of us. What must I do? Note that the question itself presupposes the reality of eternal life. Today many materialists and secularists deny the reality of eternal life because they do not believe in God. Eternal life is totally ignored in our media. Since it is a profound question, Jesus takes him seriously. In his answer, Jesus directs him to the Law – the five books of Moses. The answer quoted by the lawyer is taken from Deuteronomy 6:5 for love of God, and from Leviticus 19:18 for the love of neighbor: Love God above all things and your neighbor as yourself. Jesus comments on the answer: Do this and you will live – forever.

The lawyer's answer is the summary of the Law and the prophets, that is, the whole Old Testament. God loved us first, so we should love him in return. We should love our neighbor because God loves him and he is our brother since we are all children of God in Christ Jesus.

St. Thomas Aquinas said in this regard: "The aspect under which our neighbor is to be loved is God, since what we ought to love in our neighbor is that he may be in God" (S.Th. 2-2, 25, 1). God loves all and is in all, so all are his adopted children and they are our brothers and sisters. So we should love them in him.

The Christian love of neighbor includes everyone. Jesus says, "Love your enemies, pray for your persecutors. This will prove that you are sons of your heavenly Father, for his sun rises on the bad and good, he rains on the just and unjust" (Matthew 5:44-45). To love others means to will their good, to will their eternal salvation. We are not commanded to like everyone; that is not humanly possible because of our mutual differences and limitations.

The lawyer then moves on to another level and asks Jesus: "And who is my neighbor?" Jesus replies with the parable of the Good Samaritan which we just heard read. In contemporary language we would say that the Jewish traveler was mugged on his way from Jerusalem to Jericho. The area is desolate, a wilderness. Thieves and robbers would hide there and attack unprotected individuals. The priest and Levite are religious persons who represent the Law and the Temple in the Jewish religion. They did not help the injured man, a fellow countryman. Samaritans were considered to be pagans and heretics by the Jews and to be shunned, but it is a Samaritan who has compassion on the injured Jew. He binds up his wounds and pays two days' wages to have him taken care of at the inn.

The parable answers the question about who my neighbor is – the answer is that every person is my neighbor. Jesus' admonition to "Go and do likewise" applies to us. As a guideline we can follow the example of Jesus who said, "As I have done to you, so you do also to one another" (John 13:15).

Love of God and neighbor is essential to attain eternal life. But how do we know whether or not we love God? A sure sign of it is by having love for one's neighbor. Listen to what St. John says: "He who does not love his brother... is not of God... If anyone says, 'I love God' and hates his brother, he is a liar, for he who does not love his brother whom he has seen, cannot love God whom he has not seen" (1 John 3:10; 4:20). He also says in the same letter: "If we love one another, God abides in us and his love is perfected in us" (4:12).

Some of the Fathers of the Church saw a spiritual meaning in the parable of the Good Samaritan. They say that the one mugged and robbed is the human race, that is, all of us, because of the original sin of Adam who was deceived by the devil. The Good Samaritan, the one who rescues him, is Jesus Christ, the Savior of the world. The oil and wine stand for divine grace, and the inn is the Church. This truth is expressed in other words by St. Paul in Romans 5:8, "The love of God was shown for us in this, that while we were still sinners, Christ died for us."

Conclusion

Love of our neighbor, especially in deed, is a sure sign of our love for God, and therefore of life in God – a life of grace that is a prelude to eternal life. St. John tells us that God is love and he who abides in love abides in God – and God in him.

A good modern example of love of neighbor is in Blessed Mother Teresa of Calcutta and her Missionaries of Charity who practice the corporal and spiritual works of mercy and take care of all persons in need who come to them. We can practice the love of the Good Samarian by being good to those close to us – members of our family and those we work with. We should pray for them and help those in need when we can and in accordance with our ability.

Our Lord says, "Go and do thou also in like manner" – words addressed not only to the lawyer, but also to each one of us. God bless you.

THIRTEENTH SUNDAY AFTER PENTECOST

Readings: Galatians 3:16-22; Luke 17:11-19

Thanksgiving to God

Today we see another side of the goodness of Jesus – he cures ten lepers in response to their urgent request. At the time diseases were thought to be caused by evil spirits, so the sick turned to a holy man, a prophet like Jesus, for a cure, that is, to expel the evil spirit. The point I want to make today, based on the example of the cured Samaritan, is the importance of gratitude – giving thanks to God for the many gifts he has given us each day. We can thank him in many ways, especially by offering up the Holy Sacrifice of the Mass and by personal prayer every day. When we do a favor for someone we expect some sign of thanks, and so does God.

At the time of Jesus lepers were treated as social outcasts as protection against contagious disease (see Leviticus 13 and 14); it was something similar to our quarantine of persons who carry contagious diseases. Lepers were not allowed to enter towns or to associate closely with others. That is why Luke says "they stood afar off."

Jesus' fame had spread over Israel and the surrounding areas as a wonder worker because of his many miracles. These lepers believe that he was a man of God and could cure them. Since they were not allowed to come near to others, they cried out from a distance, "Jesus, master, have pity on us." By shouting to him they had nothing to lose and their cry meant that they had faith in him. Jesus merely said, "Go, show yourselves to the priests." The reason is that priests certified cures and then allowed the cured sick person to return to regular social life.

The ten lepers went immediately – a sign of their faith in him. On the way, they were cured of their leprosy – all ten of them. This is another sign of the divinity and divine power of Jesus because he cures them with a mere act of his will. We see from this miracle that he is the divine Physician of both body and soul.

Only one of the cured lepers, a Samaritan, turned back to praise God and thank Jesus for his cure. As we saw last week, Samaritans were despised by the Jews as pagans and foreigners. The Samaritan was grateful for his cure and gave expression to it. But the other nine did not return to give thanks to Jesus. With a note of sadness, Jesus asks, "Were not the ten made clean? Where are the other nine? Has no one been found to return and give glory to God except this foreigner?" We are saddened by ingratitude and so was Jesus.

Giving thanks to God was an important part of Old Testament ritual, especially in the Psalms, about twelve of which are Psalms of thanksgiving. Jesus praised the foreigner for doing what his Jewish companions should have done, but did not do. "Your faith has saved your," Jesus said to him as he dismissed him. His faith gained him a physical cure and also God's grace. So faith and grace are open to all – even to Samaritans and foreigners. The same lesson is taught in 2 Kings 5 in the account of Naaman the Syrian who was cured by the prophet Elisha when he washed himself in the Jordan River. The lesson is that God's love is universal – it embraces all human beings.

The ten lepers represent us. They were restored to physical health by their faith and the divine power of Jesus. Since we are sinners, we are spiritual lepers who need to be cured by Jesus. We are cured by hearing his word, by having faith in him, by receiving his sacraments which are a type of spiritual medicine, by his presence in us through grace and by adoring him in the Blessed Sacrament of the altar.

We should thank God explicitly every day for the many gifts he has given us in the past, and for what he gives us each day: life, faith, health, grace, sacraments, food, water, the air we breathe, sleep, joy, friendship, to mention just a few. We should not take these things for granted. St. Ignatius Loyola said that we should "find God in all things." Since he made all of them and sustains them in being, as his effects they bear a certain reflection of his glory.

We thank God in a very special way by offering the Mass or Eucharist to him. The word "Eucharist" means thanksgiving. We should praise and thank God with our lips, but also with our actions – for actions speak louder than words. So a life of virtue and keeping God's commandments is the best praise and thanks we can offer to God. Jesus said, "If you love me, you will keep my commandments" (John 14:23). We show our love for God and gratitude by avoiding all deliberate sin, which is the leprosy of the soul.

Conclusion

With the cured Samaritan leper let us give thanks to the Lord today and every day for all the good things, both material and spiritual, that he has given to us. A good way to do this is to use the prayer of the Psalmist in Psalm 118:1 and 29: "O give thanks to the Lord, for He is good; for His mercy endures forever." God bless you.

FOURTEENTH SUNDAY AFTER PENTECOST

Readings: Galatians 5:16-2; Matthew 6:24-33

On Putting God First

Man has both physical needs and spiritual needs because he is a composite of body and spirit. The main point of today's Gospel Reading is that God must have no rival in my life, since he created me for himself, to make me happy for all eternity. So God should come first in my life, all other things come second. Jesus tells us today, "Seek first the kingdom of God and His justice; and all these things shall be added to you."

Being weak and attached to bodily pleasures, we are tempted to put our trust in material things rather than in God – in things we can see and touch and experience, like riches, pleasure, fame and power. Jesus says clearly that no man can serve two masters at the same time. If we set our hearts on earthly things, we will forget our duty to God. "You cannot serve God and mammon" at the same time. The word "mammon" means riches and temporal things.

Here we encounter a Christian paradox: If we put money and material things first in our life, we will lose them *and* God. If we put God first, in his providential care for us God will see that we have the things we need. No man can serve two masters. Jesus is not condemning riches; he condemns an inordinate attachment to them and making a god of them. Money is good and necessary to support oneself and to support one's family. But money is not the most important thing in our life. It is a means to an end – working out our salvation.

Note that our Lord tells us not to be anxious or to worry four times in ten verses. "Worry" is an unreasonable fear of possible future evil. Faith and trust in God should rule out useless worrying and fretting about what may never happen in the future. Scripture says that faith drives out fear. Don't worry excessively about food, drink, clothing, or housing. Jesus says: Observe how God feeds the birds and animals, how he clothes the lilies of the field. In the Holy Land flowers appear in abundance at the end of the rainy season in February/March and then are burned up by the heat of the sun in two weeks.

We should learn a lesson from observing birds and flowers: God takes care of them. So will he not take even greater care of his own children, which we are? Stop worrying. Your heavenly Father knows all your needs better than you do.

Jesus says to you and to me: "Seek first the kingdom of God and His justice; and all these things shall be added to you" (6:33). There are many examples of this in the Bible; it will suffice to mention two. King David trusted God and God made him king of Judea and Israel and also the ancestor of the coming Messiah. King Solomon asked the Lord for wisdom – and he bestowed on him not only wisdom but also immense wealth and political power.

On this point *The Imitation of Christ* says, "Vanity of vanities and all is vanity, except to love God and serve him alone" (Book I, Ch. 1). St. Paul wrote to the Colossians: "Set your mind on heavenly things, not on things of earth, for you have died (to sin) and now your life is hidden with Christ in God" (3:1-3). The Church teaches us to pray in the Post Communion prayer for the Mass of the Sacred Heart that "we may learn to despise earthly things and to love the things of Heaven." The word "despise" here does not mean "hate," but rather to put in second place after heavenly things. This is a hard lesson for us to learn.

Jesus teaches us in today's Mass: Don't worry about tomorrow. Let tomorrow take care of itself. Today has enough troubles of its own. So don't make today more difficult by worrying about things in the future that may never happen. Now is the acceptable time; now is the hour of salvation. We should not waste time worrying about tomorrow. Today is all we have and tomorrow is uncertain.

Conclusion

What food for thought do we gather from today's readings? We know that God is our loving Father. He watches over us and has care for us every moment of every day. He knows all our needs. He is our beginning and our end. He created each one of us for himself. Therefore, we should put him first in our life – and not worry or fret over things which are temporary and passing. Still, we must provide for tomorrow, we must work but not be anxious about the future. This truth is summed up in those beautiful words of our Lord: "Seek first the kingdom of God and his justice; and all these things shall be added to you."

Today we should ask ourselves: Do I really believe that? Do I really put God first in my life? Do I really, deep down, seek first the kingdom of God and his way of holiness?

Remember and ponder the words of Jesus: "Seek first the kingdom of God and his justice; and all these things shall be added to you." God bless you.

FIFTEENTH SUNDAY AFTER PENTECOST

Readings: Galatians 5:25-6:10; Luke 7:11-16

Jesus Is Our Life

The theme of today's Mass is that Jesus is the life of our soul because he is the conqueror of death – death of the body and removal of sin which is the death of the soul. The four Gospels report that Jesus raised at least three people from the dead: (1) the young man of Naim in today's reading, (2) the twelve year old girl, and (3) Lazarus, the brother of Martha and Mary.

Jesus' divine power to restore the dead man to life is a sign of his power to give life to our souls by his grace which is communicated to us through the sacraments, especially Baptism, Holy Eucharist and Penance. The sacraments are instruments of Jesus' divine power by which he infuses supernatural life into our souls.

In today's Gospel we see that Jesus has compassion on the widow who lost her only son. He is her sole support, since she has lost her husband and has no other sons. In those days there was no social net in such programs as Social Security or Medicare. St. Luke tells that there was a large crowd with her, so there were many witnesses to the miracle. An unusual aspect of this miracle is that Jesus does not demand an act of faith on the part of the widow before performing the miracle. He said to the woman, "Do not weep." Then he touched the bier and commanded, "Young Man, I say to thee, 'Arise'." The man sat up, began to talk and Jesus gave him back to his mother. Here we get a glimpse of the divinity of Jesus, for with a mere word he raises the man to life. He can do and does do the same for sinners in the Sacrament of Penance.

We read in the Old Testament in the two Books of Kings that the prophets Elijah and Elisha each brought a dead boy back to life. But in their case they performed symbolic actions and pleaded with God to restore the boys to life. Jesus did the same thing with a word of command because he is the source of life both for the body and the soul. He said, "I am the way, the truth and the life" and "I am the resurrection and the life." No mere human being could say such things truthfully.

Jesus' power over physical life is a sign of his power over

spiritual life – the life of the soul. This divine life is called grace, which is the life of the soul. By his grace he gives spiritual life to millions of believers.

The Church teaches that there are two kinds of grace, both of which are supernatural. Actual grace is a passing, transient help to posit acts that are meritorious of eternal life: faith, hope, charity, humility, repentance for sins, and to overcome temptations. This grace is absolutely necessary for conversion, belief in the divinity of Jesus, and perseverance in good works.

Sanctifying or habitual grace is a permanent quality of the soul. It is a participation in the life of Christ which makes us pleasing to God. Grace makes us partakers in the divine nature, children of God and heirs of Heaven. Those in the state of grace are temples of the Holy Spirit and St. Paul says that they are now "new creatures."

Divine grace is wholly gratuitous. God does not owe it to us. It is supernatural, that is, beyond nature. Adam and Eve were created with it and lost it through their sin for themselves and also for us. Jesus Christ restored it to us through his life, passion, death and resurrection – and he gives it to us through the sacraments of his Catholic Church.

Jesus' power over physical life – in raising the young man to life – is a sign of his power over our souls by his grace. St. Augustine said that Jesus raised three persons visibly, and thousands invisibly by his grace. Jesus is our life and our resurrection and his grace is our most precious possession. It is the pearl of great price and the treasure hidden in a field. Grace is our ticket to eternal life when we die.

Through faith and the sacraments we acquire it; it grows continually through prayer, self-denial and the practice of virtue. We are all subject to physical death which is a consequence of sin. But by rejecting sin and "living by the Spirit," that is, in grace, as St. Paul urges in the Epistle for today, we embrace the supernatural life of the soul.

If because of weakness we should unhappily give in to temptation and fall into mortal sin, we can recover grace immediately by making a good confession to a priest – with sorrow for our sin and a firm purpose of amendment.

Conclusion

Because Christ has conquered death by his resurrection, we who follow him also share in his victory. He said, "Have confidence, I have overcome the world" (John 16:33). This should be a source of constant joy in our life, one of the twelve fruits of the Holy Spirit. Let us thank our Lord for rescuing us sinners from the horrors of eternal death in hell.

We should be encouraged by the words our Lord addressed to Martha: "I am the resurrection and the life; he who believes in me, even though he die, yet shall he live, and whoever lives and believes in me shall never die" (John 11:25-26). Jesus is our life, our resurrection and our hope. God bless you.

SIXTEENTH SUNDAY AFTER PENTECOST

Readings: Ephesians 3:13-21; Luke 14:1-11

He Humbled Himself

In today's Gospel Reading Jesus extols the value of humility: "Everyone who exalts himself will be humbled, and he who humbles himself will be exalted." Jesus gives a clear example of this in describing people who want the best places at table. At the time, the places of honor were those closest to the host of the dinner. Those who considered themselves important tried to take the best places. It is the humble person who takes the lowest place, not wishing to push himself forward.

The liturgy today praises the virtue of humility. Humility is the moral virtue that keeps a person from reaching beyond himself. It is the opposite of pride which is the sin of trying to be or appear to be more than one is. The humble person admits who and what he is – both his virtues and his sins. It is often pointed out that humility is truth. The word itself comes from the Latin *humus* which means earth or ground, that is, what is lowly. The truth about you and me is that we come from nothingness; we were created out of nothing by God and we are totally dependent on him every moment and everything we have, except our own sins, comes from him.

The saints, recognizing their dependence on God, consider themselves as serious sinners. Even the great St. Paul said, "I am the greatest of sinners" (1 Timothy 1:15).

Humility is both interior and exterior. Interior humility resides in the mind and heart. It is the desire to be small in one's own estimation and to attribute all good to God. The humble person judges others better than himself by comparing his sins with the virtues of others; or he compares his finite good with the infinite goodness of God. This is also the best way of avoiding the sin of rash judgment, which means that one avoids attributing bad motives to the words and actions of others.

Exterior humility refers to personal conduct that is public and visible to all. The humble person speaks modestly and courteously to all. He is helpful to others and does not manifest a haughty attitude. Humility is closely related to charity. St. Augustine said, "Wherever humility is, there is also charity."

In the Bible we find many examples of humility. Today I will mention just a few. Abraham was a humble man. He believed God and it was credited to him as righteousness. He obeyed God and even gave his nephew Lot the first choice of the land when they parted company.

Moses also obeyed God and is described as "the most

humble of men" (Numbers 12:3). The same can be said of the prophets, like Isaiah and Jeremiah. Of course Job is an outstanding example of humility.

In the New Testament the Blessed Virgin Mary is noted for her humility. To the angel Gabriel she said, "Behold the handmaid of the Lord." In the *Magnificat* she prays, "He has regarded the humility of his handmaid." Joseph, the husband of Mary, manifests humility in everything we know about him. He cared for and protected Jesus and Mary and we do not have even a single word that he uttered. John the Baptist is another model of this fundamental virtue. Of Jesus the Messiah he said, "He must increase and I must decrease."

Jesus of course is the supreme model of humility because he is the almighty God, Creator of Heaven and earth, who humbled himself to become a man in order to save us from our sins. "He humbled himself, becoming obedient to death, even to death on the cross" (Philippians 2:5-10). When he tells us to imitate him he says "Learn of me for I am meek and humble of heart" (Matthew 11:29).

Jesus rode into Jerusalem on Palm Sunday riding on a donkey, an animal of peace, and not on a horse, an animal of war. He came into this world of time and space in poverty and weakness – born in a stable on a cold winter's night. He was rejected by the Jewish leaders and nailed to a cross. We can say that he went from the wood of the manger in Bethlehem to the wood of the cross on Calvary. No one has or can surpass the humility of Jesus, the Savior of the world.

Humility is the opposite of pride. Jesus is humble and Satan is proud. St. Ignatius Loyola says that the strategy of the devil is to tempt one to riches which lead to honors which lead to pride. Pride opens one up to all other sins. The strategy of Jesus Christ is poverty which leads to contempt from others which leads to humility. Humility opens one up to all virtues. All sin is rooted in pride, while all good works and virtues flow from charity which is humble. Thus, love and humility go together.

After the three theological virtues of faith, hope and charity, humility is the most important virtue because it regulates the whole of life by submitting it to God. St. Augustine says that humility is the foundation of all the virtues.

There is also such a thing as false humility which should be avoided. Uriah Heep in the Dickens novel, *David Copperfield*, is a classic example of a man abounding in false humility. The truly humble person accepts compliments with a simple "Thank you." If you are a good cook or teacher or anything else, it is a sign of false humility to reject compliments and to say that you are no good. Whatever talents you may have come from God. The humble person thanks him and praises him for his gifts.

Those who follow Christ in faith, hope and charity will inevitably encounter contempt, rejection and humiliations like St. Paul and heroic pro-lifers who go to jail for protesting the killing of babies in the womb. When this happens, Jesus says we should "rejoice and be glad." Why? Because it makes us more like him who is the Man of Sorrows. Also, the humble person does not get angry when he is offended by others because he realizes his own weakness. And the humble person lives in peace with others, while pride causes divisions and conflict.

Conclusion

Let us listen to our Lord: "Happy are you when people abuse you and persecute you and speak all kinds of calumny against you on my account. Rejoice and be glad for your reward will be great in Heaven; this is how they persecuted the prophets before you" (Matthew 5:11-12).

That attitude is revealed in the humility of the saints and it is something for us to strive for because it makes us more like Jesus.

"Jesus, meek and humble of heart, make my heart like unto thine." Amen.

SEVENTEENTH SUNDAY AFTER PENTECOST

Readings: Ephesians 4:1-6; Matthew 22:34-46

Who Do You Say That I Am?

We are Christians because we are followers of Christ, because we believe that Jesus is the Son of God, equal to the Father, and God almighty in the flesh. This is an amazing affirmation which no other religion makes for its founder. There are many proofs for this belief in the New Testament. Today's Gospel Reading offers one of them.

Up to this point in the Gospel, the Scribes and Pharisees have been putting questions to Jesus in order to trap him into saying something blasphemous so they can condemn him to death. Their question in today's reading about the greatest commandment is their attempt to trick him into saying something contrary to the Scriptures. His answer of love of God and love of neighbor is right from the Torah and stumped them.

Now Jesus takes the offensive against his enemies and asks them two questions: "What do you think of the Messiah, that is, the Christ?" and, "Whose son is he?" Here Jesus is implicitly referring to the messianic prophecies in the Old Testament, especially Psalms 2 and 110, but also to Isaiah, Zechariah and 1 Samuel 7. Unlike his adversaries, Jesus is not trying to trap them into saying something wrong. He wants to teach them that the Messiah is more than a mere man.

Contrary to what some modern theologians say, Jesus knew who he was and who he is. He knew that he was the Messiah and the Son of God. He had this knowledge from the first moment of his conception. It is not something that dawned on him gradually as he grew to maturity.

The Pharisees reply correctly that he is David's son. As a descendant of David, he is surely a man, but in their view he is a mere man, not God in the flesh. The Messiah they were expecting was to be an earthly ruler, liberator and military leader who would drive out the hated Romans and restore the Great Israel as it was under King David and Solomon. They did not think of him as divine, as the true Son of God.

Our Lord then proves that he is the Son of God by quoting David in Psalm 110, "The Lord said to my Lord: Sit on my right hand until I make thy enemies thy footstool? If David then calls him Lord, how is he his son?" David was inspired by the Holy Spirit to make this claim for his own son who would come into the world hundreds of years after him. He could not give an ordinary man this title because the son is subject to the father. The title "Lord" from the Old Testament was given only to God whose name in Hebrew is "*Jahweh*" and in Greek "*Kyrios*."

So the inspired David attributed divine powers to his Lord who is also his son. He had equal power with the Father, for he sits "at his right hand" – a place of honor and power. He was to be a judge; his enemies would be completely subject to him – Herod, Satan, Jewish leaders, even death itself, which he conquered by his Resurrection. All of this is indicated by David saying they would be his "footstool."

What do we call him? In reality, we consider Jesus Christ to be a mere man (a) if we ignore his commands; (b) if we reject any part of his teaching, for example, regarding love of neighbor or greed or sexuality; and (c) if we fail to listen to his Church when she guides and teaches us in matters of faith and morals.

On the other hand, we acknowledge Jesus to be God almighty (a) if we love him above all things as the Bible says we should; and (b) if we love our neighbor as ourselves for his sake as St. Paul urges us to do in today's Epistle – one body, one Spirit, one Lord, one faith, one Baptism, one God and Father of all. If you would like to go into this in more depth, I suggest that you read Pope Benedict XVI's book, *Jesus of Nazareth*; there he clearly gives many arguments for the divinity of Jesus.

Conclusion

The question Jesus put to the Pharisees, he also put to Peter: "Who do men say the Son of Man is?" (Matthew 16:13). By the grace of God he believed in the divinity of Jesus and replied, "You are the Christ, the Son of the living God."

Jesus also puts the same question to each one of us to test our love for him: "Who do *you* say that I am?" May we always answer with firm faith, "You are the Christ, the Son of the living God." And may we answer his question not merely with our lips, with words, but also by our actions – by the witness of our daily lives as followers and imitators of Jesus Christ, as Mary his Mother, Peter and all the Apostles did. We do that concretely by active and effective love of God and neighbor, by keeping the Ten Commandments, by avoiding all sin, and by practicing the Beatitudes to the best of our ability. In short, we do it by leading a life of virtue.

Listen to St. Paul who urges us in today's Epistle "to walk (that is, live) in a manner worthy of the vocation in which you are called."

God bless you.

EIGHTEENTH SUNDAY AFTER PENTECOST

Readings: 1 Corinthians 1:4-8; Matthew 9:1-8

Jesus Forgives Sins

The four Gospels describe Jesus as a man of great mercy and compassion. He had compassion for both physical and spiritual suffering, as is made clear by today's Gospel Reading. The paralyzed man seeks a physical cure, but instead, at first, he receives from Jesus the forgiveness of his sins. Matthew does not tell us what those sins were. His physical illness was a symbol of his spiritual sickness, under the control of sin which is an offense against God. After the cure of his soul – the forgiveness of his sins – he receives the cure of his body.

By coming to Jesus the way he did, the palsied or paralyzed man, and his friends who helped him, manifest faith in Jesus, which in most cases in the Gospels is required for a miracle. The same event is described in a rather amusing way by St. Mark in chapter 2. There the friends take him up on the roof, remove the covering, and lower him by ropes at the feet of Jesus. They did this because the room was so filled with people that they could not gain entrance to Jesus. On this incident St. Thomas Aquinas said: "The paralytic symbolizes the sinner lying in sins. His friends represent those who, by giving him good advice, lead the sinner to God."

There is a close, even essential relationship between sin and suffering. Many of our contemporaries think it is the other way around – that sin is the result of suffering, poverty or neglect by one's parents. In reality, all suffering derives from sin and is its logical punishment, since sin is rebellion against God and man was created to know, love and serve God and so to attain perfect happiness. The source of suffering is either original sin or one's own personal sins or the sins of others.

Look at the poor paralytic. He wanted to walk, and Jesus forgave his sins. He cured his soul first since that is our most precious possession. Our body is temporal and corruptible; our soul is spiritual and immortal. The paralytic is a good image of all of us. Since we are all sinners, we all need forgiveness and reconciliation with God. That can be found only in Jesus and his Church. Jesus continues his work of forgiveness in the Sacrament of Penance. There, by contrition, confession and the absolution of the priest we attain God's grace which makes us truly his children and heirs of Heaven.

In today's first reading, St. Paul sings the praises of grace and peace with God which are bestowed on us by Jesus Christ through faith in him and repentance for our sins. As we have seen, grace was bestowed on the paralytic through the love and mercy of Jesus.

His enemies, refusing to believe, reject Jesus and accuse him of a crime against the Law, "This man blasphemes," they said within themselves. Jesus reads their thoughts, which only God can do, just as he read the heart of the paralyzed man. So, in order to prove to his enemies that he had the power to forgive sins (something invisible), he cured the sick man of his illness so that he could stand up and walk on his own (something visible).

This miracle proves his claim to be sent by God, because God does not give power to work miracles to false prophets. The proof of a true prophet is that his prophecies come true and God may work miracles through him, as he did with Elijah and Eliseus in the Old Testament.

In this dramatic Gospel event Matthew is showing us in three ways that Jesus is divine, that he is God in the flesh, that he is the incarnate Son of God. He does this (1) by forgiving sins, (2) by reading the thoughts of the Scribes, and (3) by curing the paralytic.

The total cure of the paralytic was considered so important by the evangelists that it was reported also by Mark in chapter 2 and by Luke in chapter 5.

Today's Gospel shows us that Jesus' primary concern was the spiritual welfare of the man. He cured both his body and his soul, but the soul is more important because it will live forever. There is a healthy warning here for us. Everything in our culture is directed to this world, to the material and pleasurable, to the body, to the temporal. Unfortunately, some of this mentality has also invaded the Church.

It is only the Church, however, through her preaching, her Scriptures and her Sacrament; it is only the Church that teaches us and helps us to put the right order into our lives – the spiritual first and then the material and temporal. God's law, and God's word, mediated to us by the Church, helps us to get it right. We were created for God and the Beatific

Vision. The Church, and only the Church, offers us the sure means to get there.

Conclusion

In her prayers, the Church urges us to love the heavenly realities, to put them first, and to put earthly things on a lower level. This is most difficult for us and takes great effort to accomplish. *The Imitation of Christ* tells us on this point: "Vanity of vanities and all is vanity, except to love God and serve him alone" (Bk. I, Ch. 1). Again in the same place we read: "The greatest wisdom is this – by despising earthly things to strive for heavenly glory." The idea of the primacy of spiritual, eternal goods recurs often in the liturgy, for example, in the Mass for the feast of the Sacred Heart of Jesus.

Along this line St. Paul says in Colossians 3:2 "Fix your thoughts on heavenly things, not on this earthly life." Today's Gospel helps us to nourish thoughts such as these in those words of Jesus filled with hope: "Take courage, son, thy sins are forgiven thee." Jesus forgave sins then, and he forgives them now, when we approach him with faith and repentance in the Sacrament of Penance. For this we should be very grateful and also thank God that he has by his grace called us to be members of his own Mystical Body.

NINETEENTH SUNDAY AFTER PENTECOST

Readings: Ephesians 4:23-28; Matthew 22:1-14

Infused Virtues and Gifts of the Holy Spirit

We all like a good story. That is why novels, films and TV programs are so popular. Jesus in his teaching built on that human trait and taught us many truths in the form of parables which are vivid stories constructed to make a point.

His parables are unsurpassed in all of world literature. One might mention here just a few: The Prodigal Son, The Good Samaritan, the Ten Virgins and so forth.

The parable in today's Gospel Reading, about the king who made a marriage feast for his son, tells us something about God's love for us and for all mankind.

It is clear from the Bible that many of the Israelites in the Old Testament rejected his love and his covenant by worshiping false gods – and they perished as a result of God's wrath. The patriarchs, Abraham, Isaac and Jacob, in spite of their faults, were models of faith and obedience to God. At that time, God's call to faith was directed to Abraham and his descendants.

Christ, however, came into the world to call all men to faith in him and to attain eternal salvation. That is indicated when the king says to his servants, "Go into the highways, and as many as you shall find, call to the marriage" (Matthew 22:9; see also 1 Timothy 2:4).

The meaning of the parable is that Christ is the Bridegroom and we, the members of the Church, are the bride. He invites all to enter his Church, but they must be properly dressed, that is, wearing a "wedding garment." What does he mean by the "wedding garment?"

Here it means being in the state of sanctifying grace. All who have the grace of Christ belong to him and have the right to take part in the wedding feast. This does not happen all at once. God is patient and can wait, but at the end of the world – the Second Coming of Christ in glory – the sheep will be separated from the goats, that is, those with grace will go to Heaven with Jesus and those without grace, in the state of mortal sin, will be condemned to hell for all eternity. Our Lord is giving us a fair warning.

The possession of sanctifying grace is our most precious possession – it has more value than the trillions of dollars in U.S. banks. Dollars will perish, but grace lasts forever.

As you should know from your Catechism, grace makes us friends of God, even more, his children and therefore heirs of Heaven and eternal life. Because of grace we are members of his family.

Sanctifying grace received at Baptism and increased by the other Sacraments, especially the Holy Eucharist, has some companions. Those companions are: (a) the theological virtues of faith, hope and charity; (b) the moral virtues of prudence, justice, temperance and fortitude. In addition, each baptized person receives the seven gifts of the Holy Spirit: wisdom, understanding, knowledge, counsel, fortitude, piety and fear of the Lord.

We cannot explain each of these at this time, but I will briefly describe them. The three theological virtues have God as their object and they are infused into the soul at Baptism. The moral virtues have earthly, temporal things as their object; they help us keep God's commandments and to practice the theological virtues.

The seven gifts make us capable of receiving divine inspiration and insight from the Holy Spirit. They help us to grow in virtue and to direct our lives primarily to God as our final end of existence.

Mortal sin, which drives out sanctifying grace, is a spiritual disaster. It is death to the soul – that is why it is said to be "mortal." What death is to the body, mortal sin is to the soul. The person in mortal sin loses charity, but retains faith and hope so he can repent and go to confession. The person in mortal sin also loses the seven gifts of the Holy Spirit until he repents, goes to confession and God restores him to the state of sanctifying grace.

Conclusion

As members of the Church of Jesus Christ, as members of the Mystical Body of Christ we are united to Jesus and are feasting at his marriage banquet.

For our Catholic faith, for the Holy Eucharist, for the Sacrament of Penance we should be eternally grateful to God – and tell him that every day of our life because we can never thank him enough. And we prove our love and thanks to him by keeping his commandments.

As Jesus said to his Apostles in John 14:23: "If you love me, you will keep my commandments, and my Father will love you and we will come to you and make our abode with you." May he always be with each one of us with his grace and his gifts. Amen.

TWENTIETH SUNDAY AFTER PENTECOST

Readings: Ephesians 5:15-21; John 4:46-53

Jesus' Miracles Prove His Divinity

Christianity is unique because it proclaims with certitude that a historical human being, Jesus of Nazareth, is God almighty, Creator of Heaven and earth. No other religion makes such a claim for its founder, such as Buddha or Mohammed.

One of the main points of the four Gospels is to prove that Jesus is God and therefore the Redeemer of all mankind to whom worship is due because he is Lord. Jesus claimed to be God and proved it by his miracles and prophecies. Today's Gospel Reading gives us an account of one of his miracles.

What is a miracle? It can be defined as a sensible act or effect which surpasses the powers of nature according to what is done (for example, restoring a missing limb) or the way in which it is done (for example, instant cure of blindness or cancer). A miracle is produced by the power of God to witness to some truth or to testify to someone's sanctity, such as a saint. The Church now requires at least two miracles for the canonization of a new saint.

Rationalists and atheists deny the existence of any miracles for ideological reasons. They claim that miracles are impossible because the laws of nature are immutable. They also deny the existence of a Creator God who made those laws and therefore could bypass them. The God who fashioned those laws, however, can suspend them, as Jesus and Peter walking on water.

Did Jesus really work miracles? Yes, he did. He performed hundreds of them. They are recorded in the Gospels which are true, historical accounts of the life and works of Jesus. Just to mention a few: he changed water into wine at the marriage feast at Cana; he cured ten lepers and the man born blind (John 9); he calmed storms with a word, raised three persons from the dead, and cured the official's son in today's Gospel.

Why did Jesus work miracles? He did it to prove to his disciples, and to us, that he is God and also to show his compassion and love for those who are suffering. But he did more than perform miracles; he also claimed to be God. For example, he said: "The Father and I are one"; "Philip, he who sees me, sees also the Father"; "Before Abraham came to be, I am."

In most cases, before Jesus would grant a miracle, he required an act of faith, saying something like, "Do you believe I can do this?" So one of the reasons for performing miracles was to stimulate faith in him, as at Cana and also in today's Gospel. When he allowed St. Thomas to touch him after his resurrection from the dead, he praised those who believe even though they have not seen any miracles (see John 20:29).

We should not demand more miracles than we already have as a basis for our faith. Sometimes Christians want to test God by demanding a miracle for some cure by saying, "If you cure me of cancer I will believe in you." Any prayer for a cure should always be conditional, that is, provided that it is according to God's will since he knows what is best for us. Many people pray to win the lottery and acquire millions of dollars. Perhaps if God granted that, they would end up in hell.

God's power is infinite and so is his mercy. Accordingly, miracles are still happening. The life of the Catholic Church abounds in miracles, if we only have eyes to see them – as at Lourdes, for example. The Catholic Church herself, 2,000 years old and spread throughout the world, is a moral miracle. At hundreds of thousands of Masses each day the miracle of transubstantiation takes place when mere bread and wine are changed into the Body and Blood of Christ to provide spiritual nourishment to the faithful.

In the 1980s Fr. John Houle, S.J., was miraculously cured from terminal cancer. Dying in a hospital in California, his Jesuit superior pinned on him a relic of Blessed Claude la Columbiere and prayed to him, asking for a miracle. The next morning Fr. Houle was found to be perfectly well, with no sign of the cancer. This miracle was confirmed by a Vatican official and led to the canonization of St. Claude la Columbiere, S.J. Fr. Houle traveled to Rome for the event and was present in St. Peter's Basilica when Pope John Paul II declared Columbiere to be a saint. One could recount many stories like that.

Miracles are visible signs of God's power and mercy. They are also signs or symbols of what he does invisibly in the souls and hearts of individual persons. Miracles of grace exist, if we only have eyes to see them, like the life and work of Mother Teresa of Calcutta who is now a Blessed. And the Sacraments, especially the Holy Eucharist, are all visible signs of invisible grace.

Conclusion

Our faith in God and in Jesus should be strengthened by the witness of miracles at Lourdes and other places. However, we should not incur Jesus' rebuke by demanding miracles as a condition of our faith. Our prayer should be that of the man in Mark 9:24 concerning the cure of his little son, "Lord, I believe; help my unbelief." We all need an increase of faith, for you can never have too much faith.

We should imitate the man in today's Gospel. St. John tells us: "The man believed the word that Jesus spoke to him, and went his way" – and his son was cured by Jesus in that instant.

TWENTY-FIRST SUNDAY AFTER PENTECOST

Readings: Ephesians 6:10-17; Matthew 18:23-35

Forgiveness

When we have been offended by another, especially if it is deliberate, it is hard to forgive the offense. But our Lord tells us in today's Gospel Reading that we must forgive others if we wish to have God forgive us for our sins. We might state the theme of the Mass in these words: Forgive and you will be forgiven; refuse to forgive and you will not be forgiven.

We should call to mind some outstanding examples of forgiveness. We might think of the father in the Parable of the Prodigal Son; or Pope John Paul II visiting and forgiving the man who attempted to assassinate him in St. Peter's Square. Perhaps you have not heard that, in 1945, President Chiang Kaishek of China forgave the two million Japanese soldiers who had invaded his country – and he sent them home. The supreme model of forgiveness is our heavenly Father who forgives us our sins. He loves us so much that he sent his only-begotten Son into the world to redeem us. Jesus himself, from his cross on Calvary, forgave his executioners saying, "Father, forgive them for they know not what they do."

In today's Gospel we have the parable of The Heartless

Servant. Jesus fulfilled the law of forgiveness by extending it to every person and every offense, because by his blood he made all men brother and sisters. So when Peter asked him about forgiving others seven times, which was twice what the Rabbis required, Jesus replied that we should forgive our enemies seventy times seven times, that is, without limit and always. Here Jesus is teaching us that evil should be overcome by limitless goodness, manifested in untiring forgiveness of offenses. Jesus illustrates this principle with the parable of The Heartless Servant.

The man's debt to his master is huge – many millions of dollars in our money. The servant pleaded for mercy from his master and he received it rather easily. Then, after being forgiven, he shows incredible hardness of heart when he refuses to forgive a fellow servant who owes him just a few dollars. This hardness of heart helps us to grasp the much deeper truth hidden in the parable. It gives us a faint picture of the infinite mercy of God who, in the face of the repentance of the sinner, forgives and annuls even the most grievous sins.

The parable also exemplifies the petty meanness of a man who, even though himself in extreme need of mercy, cannot forgive his fellow servant for a small transgression.

Because of our pride and the desire for revenge, and although forgiveness can cost us dearly, it is an indispensable requirement for obtaining the pardon from God of our own sins. There is no way of escape – either forgive and be forgiven, or refuse forgiveness and be condemned. After excoriating the heartless servant, the master handed him over to the torturers until he paid back all that he owed. The parable concludes in words directed to each one of us: "So also shall my heavenly Father do to you, if you forgive not your brother from your heart."

There are several dimensions to forgiveness. For example, God is always ready to forgive, but he requires repentance and conversion of heart on our part. We must sincerely ask him, "Forgive us our trespasses, as we forgive those who have trespassed against us."

Jesus forgave his executioners, even though they did not ask him for forgiveness. In imitation of Jesus, we must forgive those who injure us – whether they ask for forgiveness or not. We do not judge them – God does. There is much here for us to reflect on. We should search our own hearts to see if there is any resentment there. Do I carry a grudge against any brother or sister? Is there a secret or even explicit desire to get even? A well-known business man is reported to have said about enemies, "Don't get angry – get even." That is not the Christian way.

Every time we pray the Our Father we ask for forgiveness, "Forgive us our trespasses *as* we forgive those who trespass against us." That "as" is very important. So we should not be like the heartless servant in today's parable.

Our forgiveness of our neighbor does not necessarily mean that God forgives him. Surely he must repent for that to happen. But it means that God will forgive us when we pray, "Forgive us our trespasses."

The Sacrament of Penance helps us to secure forgiveness for our sins. All mortal sins must be confessed to a priest. This must be preceded with true contrition for our sins and a firm purpose of amendment. The acts required of the penitent for a valid confession are: contrition, confession and satisfaction.

Spiritual maturity or holiness means that we become more like God – and by his grace we are never closer to him than when we forgive those who have injured us. Even the pagan orator Cicero wrote before the time of Christ, "There is nothing that makes a man more like God than mercy." Even modern secularists and psychiatrists praise the value of forgiveness from the point of good mental health. In a well-known verse Alexander Pope said, "To err is human, to forgive is divine."

Conclusion

Love, however, is the ground from which forgiveness springs forth. Jesus said it best of all, "Love one another as I have loved you." So if you truly love your neighbor, you will truly forgive him. Today then let us all pray, "Lord, please forgive us our trespasses *as* we forgive those who trespass against us." Amen.

TWENTY-SECOND SUNDAY AFTER PENTECOST

Readings: Philippians 1:6-11; Matthew 22:15-21

God and Caesar

"Render therefore to Caesar the things that are Caesar's; and to God the things that are God's." That statement of Jesus is one of the best known quotes from the New Testament. Today let us ask ourselves: What are the "things of Caesar" and what are the "things of God"? Reflection on these divine words will help us to better understand the proper relationship between Church and State.

In many societies of the past, altar and throne have been united in one person – the king, the Pharaoh in Egypt, the Emperor of Rome. Jesus put an end to that by making a distinction between the rights of the State (Caesar) and the rights of God. They exist and operate on different levels of reality. They are not opposed to each other; rather, they are complementary, like husband and wife. The State deals with temporal things and public order in this life. It is not the ultimate reality, but is subject to the law of God. Since man's final end is to be united in love with God for all eternity, his purpose and final end is above and beyond that of the State. When there is a conflict between the two, a man must obey God rather than men, as St. Peter says in Acts 5.

In today's Gospel Reading we see that Jesus' enemies were trying to trick him into saying something that would be damaging to his good name. The Pharisees hated Rome and Roman rule and were actually opposed to paying tax to Caesar. The Herodians were fellow travelers who favored the tax, but the two groups agreed in their hatred for Jesus. So their question to Jesus about paying tax to Caesar is a trick – an apparently inescapable dilemma for Jesus. In their view, if he says No, then they will denounce him to the Roman authorities. If he says Yes, then he will anger the people who were opposed to Rome.

Jesus did not give a theoretical answer. He asked to see a Roman coin. Since they possessed and used Roman coins, it showed that they agreed in some sense to Roman rule. Someone showed him a coin and he asked, "Whose image is this and whose inscription?" They replied, "Caesar's." Then Jesus said, "Render therefore to Caesar what is Caesar's and to God what is God's."

With this brilliant insight Jesus put an end to the idea that the State is the highest expression of both political and religious authority. In our own lifetime we have seen the tendency of the State to assume absolute power over its citizens, for example, Communism and Fascism.

Since man owes his whole existence to God his Creator and not to the State, he owes limited obedience to the State, but adoration and worship to God. This takes place now, since God became man in Jesus Christ, in the Church and Sacraments established by Christ for all mankind.

Like the family, the State is a natural society willed by God. It possesses authority from God (see Romans 13 and Jesus' conversation with Pilate). This means that man has obligations to the State of loyalty and paying just taxes. But when the State commands something contrary to God's law, then one is morally bound to resist, even to death and martyrdom, as has happened many times in the past. We might think here of the Roman martyrs who refused to sacrifice to idols or the emperor, the 17th century martyrs in Japan, St. Thomas More and St. John Fisher in 16th century England. Contemporary examples include forced abortion in China, forced sterilization in India and other countries, and State mandated mercy killing for the elderly and handicapped.

God's rights over us and his objective moral law take precedence over State laws, which should always be in conformity with God's law but often are not. St. Paul says in Philippians 3:20 that "Our citizenship is in Heaven."

Yes, the State is a natural society willed by God, but so is the family which came first. The State is the result of many families banding together for mutual benefit and protection. God also established his Church as the universal means of salvation. She is a *supernatural* society which in her purpose and worship is independent of the State, for the Church's primary mission is the salvation of souls through word and sacrament. She exists to show all men how to worship God and attain eternal life after death. Social work, economics and politics are secondary and merely means to the end of saving one's soul. The first commandment is to love God above all things; the second is to love one's neighbor as oneself.

The purpose of the State is to provide an orderly, peaceful society in which citizens can provide for their own material and spiritual needs without hindrance from others.

States, however, as they grow stronger tend to assume absolute power over their citizens. We see that happening before our eyes in the USA. We have a Congress that passes laws that conflict with God's law regarding contraception, abortion, assisted suicide, stem cell research, and so forth. We have a Supreme Court that sometimes interprets the Constitution in a way that is contrary to the letter of the law.

Conclusion

As our government becomes more secular and more hostile to Christianity, Catholics are faced with some difficult decisions about cooperating or not cooperating in immoral government policies, for example, mandating contraceptives and abortion counseling in Catholic schools and hospitals; using tax monies to pay for abortions; practicing euthanasia in State-run hospitals; government monopoly in education; tolerating pornography and same-sex marriage, and so forth.

Catholics should get involved in the political process to stop immoral policies and to implement good ones, at the very least by voting for good candidates who will defend Christian morality. Men and women of good moral character, who have leadership qualities, should be urged to run for office.

Let us pray today that God will raise up by his grace more God-fearing political leaders who will "Render to Caesar the things that are Caesar's, and to God the things that are God's."

TWENTY-THIRD SUNDAY AFTER PENTECOST

Readings: Philippians 3:17-21-4:1-3; Matthew 9:18-26

Citizens of Heaven

Why did God create me? We know from the Catechism that he made me to know, love and serve him in this life and to be happy with him forever in the next life. One of the Beatitudes teaches us: "Blessed are the pure of heart for they shall see God." Deep down, that is what we all seek – to see God face to face because only he can satisfy our every desire. St. Augustine stated the same truth briefly and beautifully: "Our hearts were made for thee, O God, and they will not rest until they rest in thee."

Our present American culture, for the most part, is directly opposed to the idea of the primacy of God in our life. Our culture is materialistic, secularistic, relativistic and atheistic. On TV, radio and in the print media it tells us daily to think only of earthly riches and happiness. The fact of death is a daily topic, but not the meaning of death for the individual. The goals in this life for the worldly are riches, pleasure, power and fame. Those who promote this view of human life, according to St. Paul in today's Epistle, are "enemies of the cross of Christ." He tells us to remember that our true citizenship or homeland is in Heaven. We are on a journey or pilgrimage, and this life is like a short stay in a third-rate hotel.

St. Paul warns the Christians in Philippi about false teachers with their watered-down version of Christian doctrine which caters to the flesh rather than to the spirit. Today we are surrounded by false teachers in the media, in print, in the universities, and even in the primary schools. They treat man as a little god and deny the existence of sin. They deny the need for penance or any kind of self-denial and encourage self-gratification and pleasure seeking. In this they either reject or ignore God's rules for us on how to be a happy person in this life. The label of "cafeteria Catholicism" fits many of these false teachers to a tee.

St. Paul also says that "they mind the things of earth," that is, they are totally absorbed in material, temporal things. Elsewhere he says that "their God is their belly," that is, their absorption in the passing things of this world draws them away from the true worship of God. He also says, "Their glory is their shame," meaning that they even boast of their sins and put nice-sounding names on them. For example, as you well know, contraception is called family planning; abortion is called an exercise of free choice; adultery, fornication and homosexuality are called alternate lifestyles; lying is called misspeaking. Then we are told to be "tolerant" of these things, that is, we should not disapprove of them or condemn them as evil. We are also warned not to be "judgmental," but if we are to function as rational human beings we must judge what is real – the difference between good and evil, true and false. Certainly Jesus was judgmental when he denounced the Pharisees as hypocrites; St. Paul was judgmental when he warned us against false teachers. There is a huge difference between what is true and what is false, what is good and what is evil – and God gave us the intelligence to know the difference, at least with regard to the basics of human existence.

"Their end is their ruin," adds St. Paul. All that they prize will eventually turn to ashes and they will merit eternal damnation. But in the midst of this corruption a person always, with the help of God's grace, can live a virtuous life. St. Thomas More said: "The times are never so bad but that a good man can live in them." Evil times often produce heroic martyrs, as under the Roman Empire.

Today we should reflect on what Paul says about "our citizenship being in Heaven." By faith we know that our true and lasting home is in Heaven. We become citizens of Heaven by our Baptism which makes us partakers in the divine nature, children of God and heirs of Heaven. Thus, we are fellow-citizens with the saints. They should be our models of what it means to be a Catholic. St. Paul says today, "Be imitators of me." Why? Only because he imitates Christ.

Our Master and King is Christ. We follow him, not the false teachers of the day. They come and go; he lasts forever. God's laws are our laws because Jesus is the truth and he cannot deceive.

For a very short time we are strangers and pilgrims on earth –approximately 70 years or 80 for those who are strong, according to the Psalmist. If we are faithful and have true sorrow and repentance for our sins, our dwelling will be in our Father's house. St. Paul tells us today that Christ will come to escort us there (v. 20). He will clothe our bodies with glory because our names are registered in "The Book of Life," that is, all those who die in the love and grace of God.

Jesus is the "life," as is shown in today's Gospel Reading. He cures a woman instantly and raises a little girl of twelve from the dead. He is the source of life – both physical and spiritual. He raised three persons from the dead physically; he raises millions from the spiritual death of sin by the Sacraments of Baptism and Penance. So Jesus is the source of our physical life as our Creator and our supernatural life as our Savior.

Conclusion

When we travel abroad to some strange place or foreign country, we carry only necessary baggage; we travel light. We give our attention to important things and do not waste time on trivia. After a week or two of traveling, we look forward to being home again. Such should be the nature of our sojourn here on earth as we move day after day to our final destiny.

We should pattern our life totally on Jesus Christ who is the way, the truth and the life because our real citizenship is in Heaven. St. Paul tells us, "Stand fast in the Lord, be faithful, the time is short." Here everything passes away – everything changes. There everything is permanent. St. Augustine said somewhere, "What is not eternal is nothing."

Those who attain eternal life in Heaven can never lose it. Let us pray for the great grace of perseverance so that we will be among that number and find our names inscribed in "The Book of Life."

TWENTY-FOURTH SUNDAY AFTER PENTECOST

Readings: 1 Corinthians 1:9-14; Matthew 24:15-35

God's Final Judgment

The Church confronts us today with some very sobering thoughts in the Mass for the last Sunday after Pentecost – the last Sunday of the liturgical year. In the Gospel Reading today Jesus speaks about (1) the end of the world as we know it; (2) his Second coming at the end; and (3) the General Judgment of all mankind. That final judgment will be followed by the eternal damnation of sinners, and the eternal salvation of God's friends – those who die in the state of sanctifying grace and thereby are his children and the heirs of his kingdom. These truths concern each one of us because each one of us will be there and will be judged according to our works in this life. There is no escape.

God's future judgment of us is a truth of faith which we proclaim every Sunday in the Creed when we say, "He (Christ) will come again in glory to judge the living and the dead." The Church in her beautiful liturgy today urges us to prepare well for Judgment Day by living each day by the light of the Gospel.

Jesus tells us in today's Gospel that he will come again in glory: "Then will appear the sign of the Son of Man in Heaven coming on the clouds with great power and majesty." What is this "sign"? It is the Sign of the Cross, and he will send for his angels to gather his elect from the four winds, that is, from the whole world.

The world as we know it had a beginning, just like each one of us. It will also have an end. Jesus tells us that the world as we know it will cease to exist: "The sun will be darkened, and the moon will not give her light, and the stars will fall from Heaven..." (Matthew 24:29). God will construct a new Heaven and a new earth: "Behold I make all things new!" The world as we know it will not be annihilated – it will be transformed or transfigured, perhaps something like the body of Jesus on Mt. Tabor during the Transfiguration. What it will be like we do not know, but there will be no suffering or death, only great joy, peace and happiness forever. Perhaps it will be something like the Garden of Eden before the Fall, but much better.

Jesus foretold all these things and he cannot lie or be mistaken. What he said about the destruction of Jerusalem came true forty years after his death and resurrection, so we should believe him when he tells us about the future of this world.

From the Bible we know some of the signs of the Second Coming of Jesus and the end of the world. Theologians commonly list five signs.

Before the end, the Gospel will be preached to the whole world (see Matthew 24:14). Perhaps EWTN with its worldwide broadcasts of the Gospel is contributing to this – and perhaps hastening the end. But the Gospel has not yet reached all of China and India.

St. Paul says in Romans 11:25-32 that the Jews will be converted before the end, not necessarily each individual, but as a group.

Many will fall away from the faith through the errors and malice of false prophets (see Matthew 24:10-11).

Before the end the mysterious Anti-Christ will appear and deceive many (see 1 John 2:18-22; 2 Thessalonians 2:3).

There will be severe tribulations between peoples and nations and also in nature (see Matthew 24:9 & 29). We just heard about that in the reading of the Gospel for today.

According to Catholic doctrine, there will be two judgments for each person – the Particular Judgment and the General Judgment. The Particular Judgment takes place immediately after death for each person. This is more like a private affair when, because of our deeds during this life, the person is assigned to purgatory (for those who need purification for the temporal punishment due to sins), to Heaven for the saved, or to Hell for those who are lost – those who die in the state of mortal sin.

At the General Judgment at the end of the world all mankind, from Adam and Eve to the last person conceived, will be gathered before Christ, the Supreme Judge. The General Judgment is thought of more as a public affair in which the good and evil deeds of every person are made known to all. It will be like having your virtues and vices listed on the front page of *The New York Times*.

At that last judgment there will be only two possibilities for the eternal future of each person – Heaven or Hell. The judgment will happen very quickly, like lightning (Matthew 24:27), not like a contemporary criminal trial when lawyers and judges argue back and forth for days or weeks.

Catholic theology assigns five purposes for the General Judgment:

To manifest and glorify the goodness and providence of God.

To glorify Christ and reveal his greatness as our Redeemer.

To glorify the elect because they have been faithful to God.

To show the ingratitude of the reprobates who freely damned themselves because they rejected God who is the source of life and goodness.

To reward the saved and the damned in their bodies, since their bodies were the instruments of their salvation or damnation.

Conclusion

At the end of the liturgical year the Church asks us to reflect on the Second Coming of Christ, the End of the World, and the General Judgment. These are sobering thoughts. Their purpose is to motivate us to fidelity, to keep the Ten Commandments, to pray daily – especially to our Blessed Mother, to practice love of God and love of neighbor, to resist temptation which we are all subject to. It is absolutely certain that these things will happen – sooner or later. Jesus predicted the destruction of Jerusalem – and it happened. We must always be prepared. Remember what happened to thousands of people at the World Trade Center in New York on 9/11.

The Bible often divides men into the good and the bad, the wise and the foolish, for example, in Psalm 1 about the two ways. The foolish are the ones who ignore God and his warnings. They will be lost. The wise are the ones who hear the word of God and keep it. They will be saved. Remember the parable of the Ten Virgins – five wise and five foolish.

Let us pray for the grace to persevere in the vast army of those who hear the word of God and keep it. It is a matter of love leading to deeds, not just words. Those who do not love will be lost; those who truly love God and neighbor will be saved. Today think about that.

DECEMBER 8 – IMMACULATE CONCEPTION

Readings: Proverbs 8:22-35; Luke 1:26-28

Immaculate Mary

We live in a world full of sinners and sin, but it is at the same time a world that denies the existence of sin. Recently I spoke with a convert who told me that her parents told her that she was naturally good and that there is no such thing as sin. Why do so many people deny the existence of sin? The answer seems to be because they do not believe in God and sin is an offense against God. Therefore: no God – no sin.

But we are surrounded by sin. We see it on the evening news, we read about it in the newspaper, we hear about it on the radio – murder, theft, adultery, sodomy, lies and so forth. Sin is an offense against God, rebellion against God and putting some creature in his place. Because of original sin and concupiscence or our tendency towards sin, we are all sinners – some more serious than others.

Today on the feast of the Immaculate Conception we honor one human person, a member of our human race, who never committed a sin of any kind, who was never under the power of sin – Mary, the Immaculate Mother of God.

What is the meaning of the expression "Immaculate Conception"? First, it does not mean the conception of Jesus. It refers to the conception of Mary who was conceived in the normal way through the marital embrace of her parents, St. Anne and St. Joachim. We know from the infallible teaching of the Church, that as a result of the first sin of Adam and Eve, original sin, all human beings are conceived without sanctifying grace, the life of the soul. Because of our redemption by Jesus Christ, we can attain grace and be friends of God through Baptism, but we are conceived and come into this world without God's grace. The Church teaches us that God endowed Mary's soul with sanctifying grace from the first moment of her creation. This means that she was created in grace – she was never, not even for a moment, under the power of sin. Therefore she is called "Immaculate," that is, having no stain of sin on her soul.

"Immaculate" means to be without stain or to be stainless. Since sin is a "stain" on the soul which should be pure in the sight of God, the Church believes, based on divine revelation, that Mary was conceived without the "stain" of original sin. One indication of this is the greeting of the angel Gabriel to Mary when he said, "Hail, full of grace." The angel recognizes that she is full of grace and most pleasing to God in all that she was and did.

The prayers of today's Mass stress that Mary was "preserved" from original sin. Jesus died on the cross, rose from the dead and accomplished our redemption. He is the fountain of supernatural life for us. We partake of that life through faith, Baptism and the other sacraments. So the Church says that Mary was preserved from original sin by the foreseen merits of Jesus, her Son and her Redeemer. Mary then is the first redeemed, the first Christian; she was perfectly redeemed in every way, in soul and body and emotions. God created her as a "fitting dwelling place" for his Son. One of her many titles is "Ark of the Covenant."

Jesus came into this sinful world to crush the head of the serpent, Satan (Genesis 3:15), so Satan never had any power over him or over his mother. He was to be born of a woman who was totally free of sin. Just as God prepared a sinless Paradise for Adam and Eve, so Mary is a "second" sinless Paradise where the Son of God will dwell nine months before his birth.

The Fathers of the Church compare Mary with Eve. Eve is the mother of all the living – she is the source of both life and death. Mary is the true mother of all the living – those who live spiritually in grace with her Son. That is why she is called "Mother of the Church." Jesus gives us life through his Church and she is his mother.

We were all conceived by our parents, but with original

sin. Only Mary was "immaculately conceived." In a sense this phrase sums up the whole reality of Mary and implies our whole Catholic faith in Jesus – Son of God and Savior.

When Bernadette at Lourdes asked the beautiful lady what her name was, Mary said, "I am the Immaculate Conception." The simple peasant girl did not know what that meant – it had to be explained to her. Tennyson, the poet, got it right when he summed up the reality of Mary in these beautiful words as "Our tainted nature's solitary boast."

It follows from the above that Mary is our mother in the order of grace. In every way she cooperated with God in the redemption. To the Archangel Gabriel she said, "Behold the handmaid of the Lord. Let it be done unto me according to thy word." She was completely open to God, available, humble and obedient.

Children naturally tend to imitate their parents. We see in Mary, our Mother, all the virtues of a perfect Christian. So we should strive to imitate her just because she is our Mother. We should imitate her faith in God, her hope – knowing that God will keep his promises, her love for Jesus and her willing cooperation in his work of redemption, even going so far as to offer him to the heavenly Father on Calvary. We should strive to imitate her sinlessness to the best of our ability – by avoiding all mortal sin and all deliberate venial sins. We should ask her to obtain for us the grace to avoid all deliberate sins, so that we may be a "fitting dwelling place" for the Trinity that dwells in us through grace. Jesus is speaking to all Christians, not just priests and religious, when he says in Matthew 5:48, "You must therefore be perfect just as your heavenly Father is perfect."

Conclusion

In the New Testament Mary's last recorded words at the wedding feast of Cana are, "Do whatever he tells you" (John 2:5). If we love God, we should try to do that. When we receive

God's Son and Mary's Son in Holy Communion today, let us say to him, "Be it done to me as you desire."

O Mary, conceived without sin, pray for us who have recourse to thee."

FEBRUARY 2 – PRESENTATION IN THE TEMPLE

Readings: Malachi 3:1-4; Luke 2:22-32

Jesus Is the Light of the World

Today is the feast of the Presentation of the Child Jesus in the Temple forty days after his birth. It is also a feast of his Blessed Mother who submitted herself to the rite of purification of mothers after having given birth. She did this out of humility, though she knew that she was still a virgin and was not bound by the law of Moses.

The feast is also called Candlemas Day because on this day there is an ancient tradition of the faithful entering church carrying lighted candles as a sign of Christ as the light of the world, the one and only Savior of the world. Old Simeon refers to him as "the light of revelation to the Gentiles" because he is the Savior not just of Israel, but of all mankind.

When the Holy Family entered the Temple in Jerusalem on this occasion they went there to fulfill the law as expressed in the books of Exodus and Leviticus. That law required Mary to be purified forty days after the birth of a boy. This was called her "purification." Jesus as the firstborn son had to be offered or presented to the Lord. The prescribed sacrifice for them was a pair of turtledoves or two young pigeons. We contemplate this mystery every time we say the Joyful Mysteries of the Rosary.

This feast concludes the Christmas Season and has a joyous note about it because it celebrated Jesus' first visit to the Temple of his Father. It also has a sacrificial note because he comes to be offered to the Father as a victim for sin. Surely in his heart the child Jesus offered himself to his Father as Mary and Joseph perform the ceremonies. This is like the Offertory at Mass, but in this case the sacrifice will take place thirty-three years later on a hill called Calvary.

God had revealed to the holy old man, Simeon, that he would actually see the Messiah before he died. So the Holy Spirit directs him to the Temple at the day and time when Mary and Joseph bring Jesus for the presentation. St. Luke says that Simeon was "just and devout"; in the context this means that he was a very holy man. Simeon utters his prophecy which the Church now sings every day while praying the Divine Office: "Now thou dost dismiss thy servant, O Lord, according to thy word in peace; because my eyes have seen thy salvation... a light to the revelation of the Gentiles and the glory of thy people Israel." "Light" here means God's truth. The lighted candles today commemorate these words of the prophet. "The Glory of thy people Israel" refers to the Messiah or Savior of the world who comes from Israel.

In the first reading the prophet Malachi said that the angel of the Lord would come to his Temple and purify the priests and people of their sins. This prophecy was fulfilled by Jesus by reason of his preaching, miracles, death and resurrection. The prophecy is partially fulfilled when the Child Jesus is brought to the Temple for the first time.

Today's liturgy invites us go to meet Christ in the house of God, where we will find him in the Eucharist, where we will greet him as our Savior, where we will offer him our faith and love as Simeon did, and where we will receive him, not in our arms, but in our hearts in Holy Communion.

We come to church to meet Christ, the "Light of the World." Our Christian life of faith, hope and love should be a reflection, according to the grace given to each one of us, of the light of Christ, who is the light of the world.

Conclusion

Each one of us should be a Christian light shining in the darkness of the secular and materialistic world we live in. At each Mass we attend we should offer ourselves with Jesus to the Father, just as he did at the Presentation in the Temple. When we do that, we are real Christians, that is, true followers of Jesus Christ, the Light and Savior of the world.

MARCH 19 – ST. JOSEPH

Readings: Ecclesiasticus 45:1-6; Matthew 1:18-21

Guardian of the Holy Family

St. Joseph is one of the greatest saints of the Church, coming second only to his wife, the Blessed Virgin Mary who is the Mother of God. Joseph of Nazareth was chosen by God and called to be the husband of Mary and the foster father of Jesus, the Son of Mary and the Son of God the Father. He was chosen by God to be the guardian and protector of the Savior of the world and his holy Mother. Because of his role as head of the Holy Family, St. Joseph is now the heavenly patron of the universal Church.

The prophets, beginning with Nathan, foretold that the Messiah would be a descendant of David. That Joseph was a descendant of David is asserted in his genealogy which is provided in the Gospels of Matthew and Luke. The genealogy of Mary is not given in Scripture, but it is reasonable to assume that she also descended from King David.

St. Matthew says that Joseph was a "just man," that is, a holy and law abiding Jew. He was also a man of great faith, since St. Paul says that the just man lives by faith (Romans 1:17). We see in the prompt obedience of Joseph to the angelic directions he received that he was a man of faith and humility.

We know nothing about his pre-history or his exact age. Because of what he had to do in taking care of Jesus and Mary, he was probably a strong young man, not an old man with grey hair as he is often portrayed in some Christian art.

Joseph at first hesitated to take Mary into his home as his wife when he learned that she was pregnant. When the angel told him that the child she carried was the result of an act of God, he brought her home since she was already legally his wife.

We do know from St. Matthew's Gospel that Joseph was a carpenter, since Jesus is called "the carpenter's son." This means that he supported himself and his family by working with his hands. Workers like him at the time were usually poor, so he was poor but not destitute since he was able to travel to Jerusalem each year. In Christian art he is often portrayed holding a hammer or saw to indicate the kind of work he did.

St. Joseph was a contemplative in action. He knew that his vocation in life was to support and protect the Son of God and his holy Mother. He loved both of them and interiorly reflected on the mystery he lived with each day – his wife who was a virgin mother and the Child who was Son of the Most High. It has often been pointed out that not a single word of Joseph is recorded in the New Testament. Angels appear to him four times, and he obeys them, but he does not question their directions and he does not say anything. Joseph was the guardian of the Holy Family who was wrapped in silence. We can learn a lot about our faith by reflecting on the unusual life of Joseph of Nazareth.

Joseph was destined by God, and prepared by his grace, to be the chaste husband of Mary and foster father of Jesus. As such, he was the legal father of the Divine Savior. Joseph was close to God and lived in intimacy with him, since he held him in his arms; he clothed him; he fed him; he taught him the art and skill of carpentry. There is a tradition in the Church that Joseph died in the arms of Jesus and Mary, probably when Jesus was an adult and able to support his mother before he began his public life at the age of about thirty. The New Testament does not say anything about the death of Joseph.

Conclusion

St. Joseph is one of the greatest saints of the Church. He is the patron saint of the universal Church – and also the patron saint of many countries, like China, for example. After our Blessed Mother, he is the most powerful intercessor we have in Heaven with his divine foster Son, Jesus.

We should thank him for his beautiful example of faith, obedience and humility; we should thank him for all he did for Jesus and Mary, and for the whole Church. We should honor him because of the graces and dignity given him by God, because of his fidelity, and because of the power of intercession which he now exercises on our behalf.

St. Teresa of Avila had a deep devotion to St. Joseph and named about fifteen new convents of Carmelites after St. Joseph. She said he always answered her prayers and often advised others, "Go to Joseph."

MAY 1 – ST. JOSEPH THE WORKER

Readings: Colossians 3:14-15. 17. 23-24; Matthew 13:54-58

Go to Joseph

The feast of St. Joseph the Worker which we celebrate today is relatively recent, since it was instituted by Pope Pius XII in 1956 as a Catholic counter to the Communist May Day parades and festivities to glorify work. This feast is a complement to the traditional Mass in honor of St. Joseph which we celebrate on March 19. In Catholic countries like Austria today is a national holiday which is celebrated with parades, band music and lots of flags.

St. Joseph is one of the greatest saints of the Church, coming second only to his wife, the Blessed Virgin Mary who is the Mother of God. Joseph of Nazareth was chosen by God and called to be the husband of Mary and the foster father of Jesus, the Son of Mary and the Son of the Father. He was chosen by God to be the guardian and protector of the Savior of the world and his holy Mother. Because of his role as head of the Holy Family, St. Joseph is now the heavenly patron of the universal Church.

The prophets, beginning with Nathan, foretold that the Messiah would be a descendant of David. That Joseph was a descendant of David is asserted in his genealogy which is provided in the Gospels of Matthew and Luke. The genealogy of Mary is not given in Scripture, but it is reasonable to assume that she also descended from King David.

St. Matthew says that Joseph was a "just man," that is, a holy and law abiding Jew. He was also a man of great faith, since St. Paul says that the just man lives by faith (Romans 1:17). We see in the prompt obedience of Joseph to the angelic directions he received that he was a man of faith and humility.

We know nothing about his pre-history or his exact age. Because of what he had to do in taking care of Jesus and Mary, he was probably a strong young man, not an old man with grey hair as he is often portrayed in some Christian art.

Joseph at first hesitated to take Mary into his home as his wife when he learned that she was pregnant. When the angel told him that child she carried was the result of an act of God, he brought her home since she was already legally his wife.

We do know from St. Matthew's Gospel that Joseph was a carpenter, since Jesus is called "the carpenter's son." This means that he supported himself and his family by working with his hands. Workers like him at the time were usually poor, so he was poor but not destitute, since he was able to travel to Jerusalem each year. In Christian art he is often portrayed holding a hammer or saw to indicate the kind of work he did.

St. Joseph was a contemplative in action. He knew that his vocation in life was to support and protect the Son of God and his holy Mother. He loved both of them and interiorly reflected on the mystery he lived with each day – his wife who was a virgin mother and the Child who was Son of the Most High. It has often been pointed out that not a single word of Joseph is recorded in the New Testament. Angels appear to him four times, and he obeys them, but he does not question their directions and he does not say anything. Joseph was the guardian of the Holy Family who was wrapped in silence. We can learn a lot about our faith by reflecting on the unusual life of Joseph of Nazareth.

Joseph was destined by God, and prepared by his grace, to be the chaste husband of Mary and foster father of Jesus. As such, he was the legal father of the Divine Savior. Joseph was close to God and lived in intimacy with him, since he held him in his arms; he clothed him; he fed him; he taught him the art and skill of carpentry. There is a tradition in the Church that Joseph died in the arms of Jesus and Mary, probably when Jesus was an adult and able to support his mother before he began his public life at the age of about thirty. The New Testament does not say anything about the death of Joseph.

Conclusion

St. Joseph is one of the greatest saints of the Church. He is the patron saint of the universal Church – and also the patron saint of many countries, like China, for example. After our Blessed Mother, he is the most powerful intercessor we have in Heaven with his divine foster Son, Jesus.

We should thank him for his beautiful example of faith, obedience and humility; we should thank him for all he did for Jesus and Mary, and for the whole Church. We should honor him because of the graces and dignity given him by God, because of his fidelity, and because of the power of intercession which he now exercises on our behalf.

St. Teresa of Avila had a deep devotion to St. Joseph and named about fifteen new convents of Carmelites after St. Joseph. She said he always answered her prayers and often advised others, "Go to Joseph." That is what the Church is saying to us today on May 1: "Go to Joseph."

JUNE 24 – BIRTHDAY OF ST. JOHN THE BAPTIST

Readings: Isaiah 49:1-3. 5. 6-7; Luke 1:57-68

John the Precursor of Jesus

St. John the Baptist is a giant figure in the Gospels. He was chosen by God, and prepared by abundant graces, even being sanctified in his mother's womb before he was born – he was chosen to be the precursor of the Messiah. It was his vocation to point out to the world the Messiah and Savior of the world. At the Jordan River he proclaimed, "Behold the Lamb of God who takes away the sins of the world."

John was called by God and sent as a prophet to preach repentance for sins and to prepare the people of Israel for the coming of the Messiah. Unlike the previous prophets, Jeremiah and Isaiah who looked into the future and prophesied the coming of the Messiah, it was John's task to meet him, to worship him, and to point him out to his contemporaries. Since he goes before the Savior, he is called the "precursor." The presence of the precursor is clear proof that the Messiah is near.

The origin of John was miraculous. His mother was

barren and beyond the age of having children, but an angel told his father, Zachary, in the Temple that his wife, Elizabeth, would conceive a son who would go before the Lord to announce salvation. When John was six months old in his mother's womb, three months before his birth, the Virgin Mary, carrying Jesus in her womb, arrived to help her cousin with her pregnancy in her old age. At the greeting of Mary, Elizabeth was filled with the Holy Spirit and her son was sanctified in her womb, cleansed of original sin as happens to others when they are baptized. John was baptized in his mother's womb.

With regard to timing, please note that the Annunciation to Mary and the conception of Jesus took place on March 25. The angel told her that Elizabeth had conceived a son in her old age and was in her sixth month. So John was born three months after that – and the Church puts the feast on June 24, three months after March 25. Six months later, on December 25, Jesus is born in Bethlehem.

Like Abraham, Moses, David and the prophets in the Old Testament, John the Baptist was chosen by God and created for a special role in salvation history. He was given the grace to identify the Messiah and to point him out to others. To prepare himself for this, John spent much time in the wilderness, near the community of Qumran where the Dead Sea scrolls were found, leading a life of solitude, contemplation and penance. John was totally detached from earthly, material things and was dedicated to God and the things of God.

John prepared the people by preaching a baptism in the Jordan River of repentance for the forgiveness of sins. In order to prove that he was sent by God and was a true prophet, he quoted Isaiah, applying the text to himself. He said I am "the voice of one crying in the wilderness: prepare the way of the Lord, make his paths straight" (40:3).

Some of Jesus' disciples, like the brothers James and John, were followers of the Baptist before they met Jesus.

When John pointed out Jesus as the Lamb of God, they left him and began to follow Jesus (see John 1). When John saw Jesus walking by, he shouted out, "Behold the Lamb of God who takes away the sins of the world." The Church has the priest repeat those words at every Mass before the distribution of Holy Communion.

We see also in today's Mass that God is in control of history. What he wishes to accomplish takes place. John is the greatest of the prophets. He is the last prophet of the Old Testament and the first one in the New Testament; he grew up under the Old Law of Moses, but he saw and pointed out the Messiah and died in the time of the New Law of the Gospel. In a sense we can say that he had one foot in the Old Testament and one foot in the New. We can express the same idea by saying that he is the bridge that spans the gap between the two covenants of God with man – the Old Law of Moses and the New Law of Jesus Christ.

In praise of John, Jesus said that there is no one greater among the sons of men than John the Baptist: "Today I say to you, among those born of women there has arisen no one greater than John the Baptist" (Matthew 10:11). It was his grace and task to point out the Savior of the world, the Redeemer of mankind, the God-Man Jesus Christ who is God from God, light from light, true God from True God.

Conclusion

St. John the Baptist had tremendous faith, courage and humility, and in those virtues he is an outstanding model for us. His evaluation of Jesus is brief and profound in humility: "He must increase, and I must decrease." That is a prayer we could all profitably use. Then he made a further statement of profound humility. He said: "I baptize you with water for repentance, but he who is coming after me is mightier than I, whose sandals I am not worthy to carry; he will baptize you with the Holy Spirit and with fire" (Matthew 3:11).

John knew what God wanted him to do, and he did it. He publicly rebuked Herod for his sin of adultery and as a result he was imprisoned and died a martyr's death by beheading at the whim of a young dancing girl. He died for his faith in Jesus and for speaking the truth – truth that Herod and Herodias did not want to hear. He was finally silenced in prison by having his head cut off.

We should first admire and then imitate the faith, the courage, and the humility of John the Baptist. A sign of his greatness is the fact that the Church celebrates his birth into the world today with a first class feast. The only other births she commemorates are the birth of Jesus on Christmas Day and the birth of Mary on September 8. All other saints are commemorated on the day of their death and entrance into eternity.

John is always pointing to Jesus who is our God and our Savior. Listen to John the Baptist as he says to you: "Behold the Lamb of God; behold him who takes away the sins of the world."

JUNE 29–THE HOLY APOSTLES PETER AND PAUL

Readings: Acts 12:1-11; Matthew 16: 13-19

The Keys and the Sword

As the visitor walks towards St. Peter's Basilica in Rome, in the beautiful and massive Square designed by Bernini, he sees two huge statues about sixteen feet high, St. Peter on the left and St. Paul on the right. St. Peter is holding the keys that symbolize his authority in the Church of Christ and his index finger is pointing down at the ground, as if to say that this is my place and it is the center of the Church.

St. Paul is represented holding a sword – the sword of the Spirit and the Word of God. His finger is pointing out to the world, as if to say that the Gospel is to be preached to the whole world.

Today we celebrate the feast of these two great Apostles of the Church – both of whom were called by Jesus and both of whom were sent by him to bring the Good news of salvation to all mankind.

St. Peter has an attractive and very human personality. By trade he was a fisherman on the Sea of Galilee. He was a working man – not an intellectual or professional man. We gather from his words and actions in the four Gospels that he was inconsistent morally, impetuous, an ardent lover of Jesus Christ, and a leader of men. He asks Jesus to walk on water and Jesus grants it, but because of fear or doubts he begins to sink and Jesus saves him. He tempts Jesus to avoid his passion and Jesus severely rebukes him. Often he speaks for the whole group of Apostles without asking their permission, as in today's Gospel reading. In a crucial moment he denies that he knows Jesus, and then he bitterly repents his sin.

Because of his profession of faith in Jesus as Messiah and Lord, he is given the keys of the Kingdom of Heaven and the spiritual power of binding and loosing on earth. After the resurrection of Jesus and the coming of the Holy Spirit on Pentecost, he is a changed man. He is now a fearless preacher of faith in Jesus Christ and gives the first Christian sermon, recorded by St. Luke in Acts 2. He performs miracles by curing the sick and raising the dead. He evangelizes pagans like Cornelius and his household and accepts them into the Church (see Acts 10 & 11).

When Peter is arrested and put in jail God protects him and sends an angel to set him free, as we heard in the reading of today's Epistle. Finally, after an active and fruitful apostolate, he dies on Vatican hill, crucified upside down. He requested this because of his sins, saying that he was unworthy to be crucified the same way Jesus was.

During his ministry between 33 and about 65 A.D. Peter went to Rome, the capital of the world of the time, and established the Church there. He was recognized as the bishop of Rome. The Pope today is the successor of St. Peter and the Basilica is built over the site of his grave.

The liturgy today concentrates on Peter rather than Paul, but since the two are usually associated together, the Mass tomorrow on June 30 will commemorate St. Paul. His personality is very different from that of St. Peter. Paul was a Roman citizen of Tarsus, educated by leading scholars and himself a rabbi or teacher. As a young man he persecuted the Church, since he mistakenly thought it was a Jewish heresy. He willingly took part in the stoning of the first Christian martyr, St. Stephen.

About the year 35 Jesus appeared to Paul on the road to Damascus as he was on his way to arrest any Christians he could find. Blinded and changed by the grace of Christ, he had a change of heart and became an ardent believer in Jesus. He consulted with Peter and James and others to make sure his preaching agreed with theirs. So far as we know, Paul never saw Jesus during his earthly life. He was a mystic who was "caught up into the third Heaven," either in the body or out of the body, he did not know.

On his three missionary journeys in present-day Turkey and other countries on the Mediterranean Sea, from 49 to about 60 A.D., he established churches all over the known world. God gave him a profound understanding of the fullness of revelation – Trinity, Incarnation, grace, and God's salvific will for all in Christ Jesus. This is the "mystery" or "divine plan" that he talks about in his letters to the Ephesians and Colossians.

St. Paul was probably the greatest theologian or Christian thinker in the history of the Church, with the possible exception of St. John the Evangelist. Of the 27 books of the New Testament, 14 were written by St. Paul. St. Paul saw the connections between the Old Testament and the New Testament; that the New was hidden in the Old and the Old was made clear in the New.

St. Paul was a teacher and preacher of the Catholic faith. Devoted to his friends and converts, absolutely fearless before his enemies, Paul of Tarsus was ready to take on the whole world as the ambassador of Christ.

The Church rests on the Apostles, especially Peter and Paul, as her foundation. She rests on the authority of Peter (he has the keys), and the preaching of Paul (he has the sword).

Conclusion

Peter and Paul were both called by our Lord and sent on a mission. The same thing is true of every Christian – of you and me. Each one of us has been called by God to be a baptized Catholic. We are all called to imitate and follow Jesus Christ in our own life, and he also sends us to bring the Good News of salvation to others by our words and deeds. May the Lord Jesus grant us the grace each day to live up to our call and our mission, as St. Peter and St. Paul did.

AUGUST 6 – TRANSFIGURATION

Readings: 2 Peter 1:16-19; Matthew 17:1-9

Called to Hope

Today the Church puts before our eyes the great mystery of the Transfiguration of our Lord on Mount Tabor. Perhaps you have seen a painting of this which shows our Lord elevated from the ground, surrounded with light, and talking with Moses and Elijah who represent the Law and the Prophets of the Old Testament. Prostrate before them are the three Apostles, Peter, James and John. The same three who witness this aspect of the glory of the divinity of Jesus, will also witness his Agony in the Garden.

Matthew places this mystery after Jesus' first prediction of his passion, death and resurrection. The same Gospel Reading is found for the Mass of the 2nd Sunday of Lent: to encourage, strengthen and inspire hope in attaining the happiness of Heaven, by the grace of God, through suffering to glory, just like Jesus.

In his Transfiguration Jesus allows some of his divine glory to shine through his humanity. The "cloud" is a visible sign of the presence of God, as was the case in the Old Testament. The disciples are overcome with fear, because the experience of the majesty of God makes one realize that he is a creature and totally dependent on God. They hear the voice of the Father saying, "This is my beloved Son in whom I am well pleased. Listen to him." After the Transfiguration Jesus touched them and told them not to be afraid – they are not in danger.

This vision of Jesus' glory was meant just for these three Apostles. So on the way down the mountain Jesus charged them saying, "Tell the vision to no man till the Son of Man be risen from the dead."

Let us consider the three disciples. They see Jesus in glory talking with Moses and Elijah. St. Luke says they were talking about his passion and death which was soon to take place in Jerusalem. They hear the voice of God and are afraid, but they are also filled with joy. Peter even had the courage to say to Jesus, "Lord, it is good for us to be here."

The purpose of the Transfiguration before the disciples was to strengthen them for the coming trial of his passion and death, and for their own future suffering and death as his witnesses to the world. It was also directed to increase their faith, hope and love for him.

Hope is a virtue we all need and it is born from a living faith in the divinity of Jesus Christ. Faith not only makes us certain about the existence of God, but assures us that God is goodness, beauty and infinite love who wishes to give himself to us as our possession and eternal happiness. This faith gives rise to hope of possessing him.

In general, natural hope is the expectation of attaining in the future some good – marriage, a new home, a job, a new automobile. Natural hope is based on one's own efforts, or good luck, and ceases once what is desired is obtained.

Supernatural hope is different. It is the theological virtue by which we trust with complete certitude in the attainment of eternal life and the means necessary for reaching it. God has promised it and he will certainly give us the means if we do our part. Hope in turn gives rise to love of the known and expected good.

Just as we cannot believe in what we understand, for example, that two plus two equals four, so there is not hope for what we already possess. But once we possess the hoped for good, we feel a sense of joy and satisfaction. The saints are joyful because they are united to God who is the source of all good. There are no sad saints.

There are two sins against the virtue of hope: despair and presumption. By despair a person ceases to hope for his personal salvation, either because he thinks God does not exist or, if he does exist, that he will not pardon his sins. Despair results from a life of sin, rebellion against God and rejection of his grace.

The sin of presumption means that a man takes God for granted, that he expects to attain Heaven without using the means to get there, that God is such a "good guy" that he would never send anyone to hell.

Conclusion

The three disciples saw Jesus' glory – they rejoiced and they were also afraid. The purpose of seeing that glory was to strengthen their faith in him because he had to go through his passion and death to reach his glorious resurrection. The three disciples represent each one of us – we believe in him, hope in him and love him. If we are faithful to him and persevere in the face of suffering, that is, if we follow him and hope in him, he will not fail us. He will be with us in this life and will take us to share in his glory when we die. I conclude with these consoling words of Jesus: "If you love me, you will keep my commandments, and my Father will love you, and we will come and take up our abode with you" (John 14:23).

NOTE: For more material on the Transfiguration see the homily for the 2nd Sunday of Lent.

AUGUST 15 – ASSUMPTION OF THE BLESSED VIRGIN MARY

Readings: Judith 13:22-25; 15:10; Luke 1:41-50

Body and Soul in Heaven

Today is the feast of the Assumption of the Blessed Virgin Mary into Heaven, both body and soul. In the early Church it was also called her "Dormition." In Jerusalem, on Mount Sion, there is a Benedictine church called "Dormition Abbey." On the lower level there is a shrine to Our Lady. In a life size statue she is shown in the prone position, sleeping, waiting to be assumed into Heaven.

This liturgical feast can be traced back to the 6th century in Jerusalem and the 7th century in Rome. The word "assumption" means being taken up into Heaven by the power of God. Because she was totally sinless, the Mother of God and the cooperator in our redemption, Mary received a special privilege of being assumed body and soul into Heaven at the end of her life. The definition does not say that Mary died, but most theologians argue that she did die before her assumption and in this she imitated her Son.

Mary's assumption reminds us that our permanent abode is not on earth but in Heaven where she, with her divine Son, has preceded us with her full human nature. The assumption reminds us to live ever intent on heavenly things. This is difficult in our world which is so materialistic and absorbed with the here and now – all of which is passing away. We seek permanence but do not find it in this world of time and space; it is found only in God.

At the end of her life, probably shortly after her death, Mary was assumed body and soul into Heaven. Since she was totally sinless, God did not allow her body to see corruption, as happens to all dead persons. She received this privilege because she was chosen by God from all eternity to be the Mother of God – the Second Person of the Blessed Trinity. By the grace of God ("Hail Mary, full of grace") she was the Immaculate Virgin, Mother of God. So the devil never had any power over her since she never committed any sin, not even a venial sin.

Mary Immaculate, like Jesus, is our model. She shows us the way we must follow to get to Heaven:

By detachment from earthly things: she was free from all sin and from all inordinate attachment to the things of earth;

By flight towards God: In her Assumption Mary teaches us to fly towards God. Her whole heart and soul were dedicated to God alone; she loved God with her whole heart, mind, soul and strength;

By union with God: Mary's Assumption speaks to us of the Beatific Union with God as our final destiny. Her Assumption confirms us in this beautiful truth: We are created for and called to personal union with God. We should keep our eyes on her – she will show us the way. She is our model. Mary is the First Christian, the Perfect Christian. The more we imitate her, the closer we come to God.

Conclusion

God has promised that we also shall rise from the dead, glorious and immortal, on the last day when Christ comes again in glory. This promise has an important condition attached to it: We must die in the state of sanctifying grace, as Mary did. For that we need the grace of final perseverance which we should pray for every day.

Where Mary is now with the glorified Christ, we hope also to be one day. So our religion is a religion of hope because our God is a God of hope. If we keep the commandments – all of them – persevere in prayer, and imitate Mary in her faith and humility, God in his mercy and goodness will give us the grace to share in Mary's glorious Assumption into Heaven.

Today we pray: "O Mary, conceived without sin and assumed body and soul into Heaven, pray for us who have recourse to thee."

SEPTEMBER 14–EXALTATION OF THE HOLY CROSS

Readings: Philippians 2: 5-11; John 12:31-36

The Tree of Life

The cross is something that we as Catholics are very familiar with. It presides over our churches, schools, hospitals and monasteries. In most churches it is used for adornment above and below. It clings to the walls of our homes, bedrooms and even kitchens. Women adorn themselves with expensive golden crosses and men can be seen wearing metal or wooden crosses on their chests, suspended from a cord or chain around the neck. Thus we are familiar with the idea that the cross is a sign of faith, a sign of the triumph of good over evil.

But there is also something forbidding and ominous about the cross. After all, the cross was used by the Romans as an instrument of torture and death, but only for non-Romans. Crucifixion was such a hideous death that it was forbidden by law to apply it to Roman citizens. That is why St. Paul, a Roman citizen, was beheaded instead of being crucified like St. Peter. When we reflect, for example, during Holy Week, on the detailed suffering and torture in crucifixion it makes us shudder with abhorrence and fear. Jesus embraced that death out of love for us.

We all know that Jesus Christ died on a cross bathed in his own blood on that first Good Friday many centuries ago. According to the Father's plan (Acts 2:23) Jesus effected our salvation by dying on the cross. In fact, on a number of occasions he predicted how he would die. In John's Gospel we read: "When I am lifted up from the earth, I will draw all men to myself" (12:32). In today's Gospel reading John touches on the same idea from a different angle: "Just as Moses lifted up the serpent in the desert, so must the Son of Man be lifted up, so that all who believe may have eternal life in him." Thus salvation, redemption, grace, eternal life – no matter how you wish to express this divine reality – has been given to us *through the cross of Jesus Christ.* Accordingly, the cross is a sign both of shame and of triumph. Looked at from the perspective of the Last Supper it inspires abhorrence; after the resurrection of Jesus it is seen as a sign of glory.

The cross is a paradox – a point that is made even in the title of today's feast: Exaltation of the Holy Cross. It is both death-dealing and life-giving. Death came into the world through the sin of Adam, because he ate of the fruit of the forbidden tree. The tree of the cross was an instrument of death. But it is also a source of spiritual and eternal life for those who believe in Jesus Christ who came to his glory with the Father in Heaven through the wood of the cross.

The central place of the cross in Christian belief is strongly emphasized by St. Paul. One of his most famous passages on Jesus is contained in the Epistle for today. St. Paul says that Jesus obediently accepted death, *even death on a cross,* and "because of this God highly exalted him, and bestowed on him the name above every other name...

Jesus Christ is Lord." Paul was taken up with the mystery of God's plan to save mankind through Jesus' sacrificial death on the cross (see Ephesians 1:3-4). For him the cross is "the power of God" (1 Corinthians 1:18) and "the wisdom of God" (1 Corinthians 2:2). Paul's one boast is the cross of Jesus Christ: "May I never boast of anything but the cross of our Lord Jesus Christ! Through it the world has been crucified to me and I to the world" (Galatians 6:14).

The cross was foreshadowed by the tree of the knowledge of good and evil in Paradise. Reference to this is made in today's Preface where the Church prays that "he who overcame by the tree (that is, Satan) might also be overcome on the tree" of the cross. It was also foreshadowed by the uplifted bronze serpent as we read in Numbers 21. For, just as by the power of God the Israelites who looked upon the bronze serpent were saved from the deadly poison of the snakes in the desert, so also those who look upon the crucified Lord Jesus with faith "have eternal life in him."

Over the centuries Christians have developed an abundance of symbols that stand for the faith: the sacraments, the Mass, the Apostles and so forth. But the cross is the most common of all Christian symbols. Making the sign of the cross on the forehead with the thumb or forefinger was already customary in the 2nd century. Later, in order to signify belief in the Trinity, three fingers were used to trace the cross on the forehead and the breast. The sign of the cross as we now make it has been traced back to the 5th century.

The sign of the cross is used in many different ways in the liturgy. Depending on where and how it is used it will signify that one belongs to Christ or that one is invoking the power and grace of God. In exorcisms it is used repeatedly to invoke the power of Christ over the devils. And of course it is used in all types of blessings.

Because we were redeemed by Jesus' death on the cross we owe a special debt of reverence to the cross. Thus the Church directs us to genuflect before the cross on Good

Friday and to reverence it by kissing it. But even though this takes place on Good Friday it should be noted that the motif of the veneration is one of glorious triumph.

Every time we make the sign of the cross we are professing belief in Jesus Christ, in his eternal Father and in the life-giving Holy Spirit. The cross is a sacred symbol of our faith and it should be treated in a sacred manner. Every Catholic home should have at least one crucifix in a place of honor.

Perhaps the theme for today's Mass is best summarized in that beautiful prayer that we utter together at each of the fourteen Stations of the Cross: "We adore thee, O Christ, and we praise thee, because by thy holy cross thou hast redeemed the world."

LAST SUNDAY OF OCTOBER – CHRIST THE KING

Readings: Colossians 1:12-20; John 18:33-37

The King of Hearts

The feast of Christ the King was instituted for the whole Church in 1925 by Pope Pius XI. It is set for the last Sunday of October, shortly before the feast of All Saints. Americans do not have experience of kings and queens, except in books and films. A king is a ruler who has supreme authority over a particular territory. His power over his people is complete: executive, legislative and judicial.

A kingdom is the area over which, or within which, the king exercises his authority. The New Testament speaks of the kingdom of God or the kingdom of Heaven to signify the reign of God's love over individual persons. But God's kingdom or reign is completely different from all earthly kingdoms. It is not political, but spiritual and over the minds and hearts of persons. When Pilate asked Jesus if he was a king, Jesus answered by saying Yes, but "My kingdom is not of this world." One enters the kingdom of Christ by faith, remains in it by love, and perseveres in it by hope.

Jesus Christ is King because he is God Almighty, the Creator of Heaven and earth. His kingdom is present in the world now. Where is it? It is found in the Church which is the Mystical Body of Christ. We cannot see it with our eyes, but it is "within us" or "in our midst," as Jesus says in Luke 17:21.

Because of sin and error God's kingdom is now incomplete. It will be complete or perfect at the Second Coming of Christ. At the end of the world Jesus will finally triumph over sin, Satan and death.

There are many intimations in the Old Testament of the coming king or glorious Son of Man. Through the Old Testament prophets God promised a future good king, the anointed, the Messiah, the Son of David. It was predicted that the anointed king would rule over his people with love, peace and justice.

In Daniel 7 the mysterious "son of man" means first of all the people of Israel. Later it was applied to the Messiah. It was said that his kingdom would last forever. Jesus, by referring to himself as the son of man, alluded to the prophecy of Daniel. It also has been applied to him by the Church, especially in reference to his Second Coming. This phrase always has a religious sense: Jesus is a king of love, a king of hearts. He rules by the power of truth and by his love for us, especially on the cross which is his throne. He has merited to be called "the King of Truth."

Jesus is King of kings and Lord of lords by reason of his divine sonship, as we read in the book of Revelation. He demonstrated his love for us on the Cross when he atoned for the sins of mankind by the shedding of his blood. He has also made us "a royal nation of priests" in the service of God the Father, that is, in his name all Christians can offer sacrifice to God the Father in what is now called the priesthood of the faithful.

Jesus is the transcendent God Almighty, the alpha and the omega, the beginning and the end – the One who is, who was and who is to come.

In today's Gospel we contemplate a great difference between Jesus and Pilate. Pilate asked Jesus, "Are you the King of the Jews?" The ensuing dialogue between the two revolves around what it means to be a king and who is king. Pilate and the Jewish leaders are thinking in terms of an earthly king with political power and control of an army to enforce his will – someone like Caesar in Rome. Jesus flatly rejects the notion of an earthly king, but he still claims to be a king – a King of Truth. He said, "Yes, I am a king; I was born for this; I came into the world to bear witness to the truth; all on the side of truth listen to my voice" (11:37).

With this reply to Pilate Jesus gives a new meaning to the idea of a king. He is king in a spiritual or religious sense. He rules over the hearts of men by faith, hope and charity. So Jesus Christ is king on two levels: (1) by his divinity he is our Creator and Redeemer; (2) by his humanity he saved us by his suffering and death on the cross.

Today on the last Sunday of October we adore Christ and honor him under the title of "Christ the King." According to the special Preface for this Mass, the Church prays that his kingdom is "a kingdom of truth and life... of holiness and grace... of justice, love and peace."

Jesus wants you and me, and every human person, to be a member of his kingdom. We enter it by believing in his word, by loving him and by placing our hope in him. We remain in it by keeping his commandments – by every day practicing love of God and neighbor.

We must remember that Jesus is a different kind of King, that he is a King of Hearts. He rules us through truth and love, not by force and intimidation.

In his Gospel, St. John links Jesus' kingship to his passion. "The cross is Christ's royal throne; from the cross he stretches out his arms to draw all men to himself, and from the cross he rules over them by his love. For him to reign over us, we must allow ourselves to be drawn to him and to be conquered by his love" (*Divine Intimacy*, IV, p. 238).

The Mexican Jesuit Martyr, Padre Pro, did what Jesus did. With his arms extended in the form of a cross, before being executed by a firing squad in 1927, he shouted out as loud as he could, "*Viva Cristo Rey*" – Long Live Christ the King! Today that should be our prayer also. Because he is my Creator and Redeemer, may he reign over my heart forever.

NOVEMBER 1 – ALL SAINTS DAY

Readings: Revelation 7:2-12; Matthew 5:1-12

Lord, I Long to See Your Face

Today we honor, and invoke, all the saints in Heaven – not just the canonized saints but all who have attained the face-to-face vision of God. How many saints are there in Heaven? We do not know. St. John says it is "a huge crowd which no one could count from every nation...." We may hope that all make it, but we do not know for certain. Our Lord says in Matthew 7 that the gate is narrow and the way is difficult that leads to life, so we have to be diligent in working out our eternal salvation. We are all part of the people of God – the communion of saints – so we ask those in Heaven to pray for us and help us to join them.

St. John says in the book of Revelation that there is "a seal on the foreheads" of the blessed in Heaven. This is the baptismal character which all receive with the sacrament. Only those with this seal, given with Baptism or in some other way known only to God, are admitted to Heaven. The number of the saved of 144,000 is not intended to be an exact number. In scriptural terminology it means a perfect number – all those who are saved. This number is arrived at by multiplying 12 by 12 by 1000 – a perfect number.

The saints are described by St. John as wearing long white robes and carrying palm branches in their hands. The white robes stand for sanctifying grace and the palm branches are a sign of victory over sin, Satan and death. They sing in unison, "Salvation is from our God... and from the Lamb (Jesus). This means that God the Father is the source of grace and sanctification but it is granted through Jesus Christ the Lamb who merited it for us by his passion and death.

They also sing, "Amen. Praise and glory...." Adoration of God is the primary occupation of the saints. Who are they? They are the ones who survived the great period of trial. They washed their robes (souls) and made them white (grace) in the blood of the Lamb; that is, they believed in him and followed him.

In his first letter St. John says that we are children of God, with all that implies: grace, adopted sonship, and heirs of Heaven. What we shall be in the future we do not now know, but we shall be like him because we will see him as he is. Everyone who has this hope keeps himself pure as he is pure, that is, sinless. The faithful Christian does the will of God, keeps the commandments, practices love of God and neighbor, and follows his own grace of vocation. God's call goes out to all, but it is different for each person.

If we want to share in the glory and happiness of the saints in Heaven, we must follow in the footsteps of Jesus, as the saints did, and imitate them. St. Paul urged his converts to imitate him, since he imitated Christ. Jesus' program for joining the saints in Heaven is clear: practice faith hope and charity, receive the sacraments, keep the commandments, and live the Beatitudes to the best of your ability and the grace you receive.

The Beatitudes are eight steps to Heaven, like the 12-steps of Alcoholics Anonymous, only they are more basic. These attitudes are diametrically opposed to the values of the world. Those who follow them will suffer, in one way or another, persecution and trials from worldly persons and sometimes even from members of their own family.

The Beatitudes are opposed to the seven capital sins:

The poor in spirit are a rebuke to the proud in heart;
Being merciful is opposed to avarice;
Mourning for one's sins vs. mourning at the good fortune of others (envy);
The meek and the peacemakers clash with those who are driven by anger, revenge and violence;
Hungering for righteousness contrasts with those satisfied with sloth;
The pure of heart give example to those filled with lust;
Courage under persecution opposes self-indulgence and gluttony.

The Beatitudes are Jesus' roadmap to Heaven and to blessedness. The saints all traveled that road and we must travel it if we want to reach the goal of Heaven.

Years ago a successful Catholic lawyer, who had a large family and many friends, one day told a group of friends what his philosophy of life was: (1) always tell the truth; (2) keep the commandments; and (3) practice the Beatitudes. He kept that philosophy and was amply rewarded by God.

Conclusion

In order to endure suffering, trials and persecution in a meritorious way, we need strong motivation. Filial love of God and the hope of gaining Heaven give us the motivation we need. Today we commemorate and contemplate the happiness of all the saints in Heaven – canonized and not canonized. We should ask ourselves today: "Lord, do I long to see your face?" We can ask the saints today to intercede for us, to secure for us the grace of longing for holiness. In the Eucharist we are close to Jesus for a few minutes in a special sacramental way. Today, when we receive him, let us look heavenward and say, "Lord, I long to see your face."

NOVEMBER 2 – ALL SOULS DAY

Readings for the second Mass: 2 Maccabees 12:43-46; John 6:37-40

Pray for the Faithful Departed

"It is therefore a holy and wholesome thought to pray for the dead that they may be loosed from sins." This text from the Second Book of Maccabees is important in Church history as a proof for the existence of purgatory.

Human beings, you and I, are endowed with the great power of memory. We can remember past events – good days and bad days, relatives, friends, books we have read and things learned in school. All Souls Day is the day the Church sets aside to remember all the faithful departed – to offer Masses for them and to pray for them, whether they died recently or long ago.

In today's Epistles we read that Judas Maccabeus won a military victory over Gorgias, but some of his soldiers were killed in the battle. When they were buried it was noted that they were carrying pagan charms or images of pagan gods, which was a sin. But they were noble soldiers because they died fighting for Israel and the Lord. Judas took up a collection for them and sent 12,000 drachmas, a large sum, to Jerusalem to pay for sacrifices to be offered to the Lord for them. "If he had not expected them to rise again, it would have been foolish to pray for the dead." The implication is that they need some purgation because of their sin. This raises the question of the existence of a place or state of purgation which we call "purgatory."

Purgatory is defined as the state or condition in which the departed souls of the just are purified after death and before they enter Heaven. Because of the holiness of God, nothing unclean can enter into his presence. So purgatory is for those persons who have venial sin on their souls when they die, and for the temporal punishment due to forgiven mortal sins for which adequate satisfaction has not been made by prayer and penance. When they have made satisfaction, they leave purgatory and go to Heaven.

It should be noted that purgatory, therefore, is a state of hope and love, for those detained there know for certain that they will go to Heaven. On the other hand, hell is a state of hate and despair.

The existence of purgatory is an article of Catholic faith. It has been affirmed and taught by many Fathers of the Church, by saintly theologians like Thomas Aquinas, and by at least four councils of the Church: Lyons in 1274, Florence in 1438, Trent in 1563, and Vatican II in 1965. In addition to 2 Maccabees, many Fathers interpret the words of Jesus in Matthew 12:32 as referring to purgation in the next life: "Anyone who says a word against the Son of Man will be forgiven; but anyone who speaks against the Holy Spirit will not be forgiven either in this world or in the next." This implies some purgation and therefore purgatory.

After the particular judgment of each person immediately after death, those who are sent to purgatory know for certain that they are saved and in this they rejoice. But since they need cleansing from the consequences of sin, they are denied the vision of God until such time as they are fully cleansed. This separation is most painful to them, since their whole being longs to be untied to God.

We are not certain about the nature of the punishment in purgatory. The Church does not teach officially that it is fire, even though many Fathers of the Church, Catechisms and preachers speak of "the fires of purgatory." The councils speak of "purifying punishments." Whatever it is, it is painful and produces suffering – if it is not physical fire, it is something like fire.

Suffering in purgatory is not the same for all because it is proportioned to each one's sinfulness and need of cleansing.

The teaching about purgatory is based on the doctrine of the Communion of Saints and the Mystical Body of Christ. All those who are in the state of sanctifying grace are living members of the Body of Christ – those on earth, those in purgatory, and those in Heaven. So we on earth can help those in purgatory with our prayers and penances. By the constant belief and practice of the Church we know that the souls in purgatory can be helped by the prayers and penances of the faithful on earth. This ties in with the doctrine on indulgences. An indulgence is defined as the extra-sacramental remission of the temporal punishment of sin remaining after the forgiveness of the guilt of sin (see Ott, *Fundamentals of Catholic Dogma*, p. 441).

Indulgences are gained by performing certain prayers and good works, like reciting the Rosary, making the Stations of the Cross, and saying prayers to which indulgences are attached by the Church. In order to shorten their stay in purgatory, we are urged to pray for the souls in purgatory, to offer up Masses for them, and to offer up our sufferings for them. We do not know how long individuals are detained in purgatory. We know that martyrs go straight to Heaven – no purgatory for those who shed their blood for Christ. St. Teresa of Avila said that she knew of only two persons who went straight to Heaven after their death.

Plenary indulgences, which provide the full remission of the temporal punishment, are important and can be gained during November and at other times. The conditions for gaining a plenary indulgence are: (1) intention to gain it; (2) performance of the work; (3) communion on that day; (4) confession eight days before or after; (5) no attachment to venial sins. A plenary indulgence can be gained only once a day.

Conclusion

Today and every day we should remember our departed relatives and friends, and all the faithful departed, in our prayers. For, "It is a holy and wholesome thought to pray for the dead, that they may be loosed from their sins."

The story is told of a holy Chinese missionary who asked to be buried in the cemetery of the Benedictine nuns in Bristow, Virginia. While making a retreat there, he noticed that the sisters went every day to the cemetery to pray for the dead nuns, so he wanted to be buried there to profit from their prayers, in case he was detained in purgatory.

Belief in purgatory is based on belief in eternal life and the final resurrection of the body at the last day. If we are generous in praying for the poor souls in purgatory, we may hope that others will remember us and pray for us when we go to purgatory to suffer the temporal punishment for our own sins. "It is a holy and wholesome thought to pray for the dead, that they may be loosed from their sins." God bless you.

NOVEMBER 9 – DEDICATION OF THE BASILICA OF ST. JOHN LATERAN

Readings: Revelation 21:2-5; Luke 19:1-10

The House of God and Gate of Heaven

We have a Pope who is the Vicar of Jesus Christ on earth and head of the Church. Is there one Catholic Church building which occupies the first place among all Catholic cathedrals and churches? The answer is Yes, and it is the Basilica of St. John Lateran in Rome, which is also called "The Church of Our Savior." It is one of the four station churches in Rome, along with St. Peter's, St. Mary Major, and St. Paul Outside the Walls. Any pilgrim, by visiting these four churches, can gain a plenary indulgence.

St. John Lateran is the Pope's cathedral church in Rome. St. Peter's is his chapel. For over 1000 years the Popes lived in a palace next to this church and five ecumenical councils were held there. On the façade of the church is the inscription: "The Mother and Head of All Churches in the City and the World." It is in this church, not in St. Peter's, where the Pope announces important events that concern the whole Catholic Church. So, for example, it was in this church that Pope John XXIII announced the convening of the Second Vatican Council.

A church is a sacred place set aside from worldly affairs for the worship of God. It should be beautiful, different from secular buildings, and suitably adorned. No business or secular affairs are allowed there because it is the House of God. Michael Rose in his book on Catholic architecture, *Ugly as Sin* (2001) says that there are three characteristics of a Catholic church: Permanence, verticality and iconography. Certainly St. John Lateran is a good example of all three. We treat churches differently from the way we treat other buildings because God is present in a special way in his church. He is there to sanctify us and save us – so it is a holy place.

We all come into this world with original sin on our souls which we have inherited from Adam. Through Baptism in our church that sin is removed and we receive the grace of God which makes us his children and members of his family. There we enter into communion and friendship with God our Creator. The sacraments are normally administered in a church, with the exception of the Anointing of the Sick which is often given in a hospital or at home.

The main divine action in church is the offering of the Holy Sacrifice of the Mass. It is the sacramental representation of the bloody sacrifice of Jesus on Calvary 2000 years ago during which we can receive the Body and Blood of Christ in the Holy Eucharist. The Eucharist is preserved in the tabernacle so Jesus is always present in our churches under the appearances of bread and wine. He is there to comfort us, to receive our prayers, and to save us as he saved Zacchaeus when he visited his home.

God was present spiritually in the Temple in Jerusalem, in the midst of the Jewish people until its final destruction by the Romans in 70 A.D. He is now present sacramentally, Body, Blood, Soul and Divinity, in the Eucharist in the tabernacle of Catholic churches. When we want to pray, to talk to God, to ask for help, to ask for forgiveness, the place to go – if possible – is before the Blessed Sacrament in a church or chapel.

In a similar way, every baptized Catholic is a temple of the Holy Spirit through the possession of sanctifying grace and the indwelling of the Trinity in the soul of the just person. St. Paul wrote to the Corinthians: "Do you not know that you are God's temple and that God's Spirit dwells in you?" (1 Corinthians 3:16). In today's Gospel we read that Jesus entered the house of Zacchaeus, who was a public sinner, to have a meal with him and his friends. The result was repentance on the part of Zacchaeus, restoration to friendship with God, and great joy. Jesus went into the house of Zacchaeus and saved him. That is what we should desire – that Jesus take up his abode with us. He will do that if we keep his commandments, especially love of God and love of neighbor.

In today's Epistle, St. John gives us a wonderful description of Heaven – the Holy City, the New Jerusalem – which is the dwelling of God with man. Being a member of the Church now is an anticipation of Heaven. Then there will be no more suffering and tears and death – only joy and eternal happiness that can never be lost.

Conclusion

Our present state of sanctifying grace – which should never be tarnished or lost by sin – is the beginning of glory. It means that God is present within us right now. Grace is our most precious possession. Jesus tells us clearly: "If you love me, you will keep my commandments, and my Father will love you and we will come to you and take up our abode with you" (John 14:23). May the Lord say today to each one of us what he said to Zacchaeus as he sat in his house: "Today salvation has come to this house.... For the Son of Man came to seek and to save what was lost." Amen.

A SUPPLEMENTARY SERMON FOR USE ANYTIME

The Holy Sacrifice of the Mass

Today I would like to offer you a brief explanation of the nature of the Holy Sacrifice of the Mass – what it is and what happens at Mass. The Mass is the most important act of worship of the Catholic Church. The altar where it takes place is the most important place in a Catholic Church. In most churches the eye is directed to the altar by the way the church is built. In large basilicas the dome is over the altar to signify its importance. Protestant churches have a pulpit but not altar because they do not offer sacrifice.

I. The Structure of the Mass

There are two main sections to the Mass: The Liturgy of the Word and The Liturgy of the Eucharist. The Liturgy of the Word has the following parts: (1) Prayers at the foot of the altar; (2) Introit, Kyrie, Gloria, Collect Prayer; (3) Epistle, with Gradual and Alleluia; (4) Gospel and Sermon; (5) Nicene-Constantinople Creed.

The Liturgy of the Eucharist has the following parts: (1) Offertory in which we offer bread and wine; (2) Consecration. Speaking in the person of Christ the High Priest, using his same words the human priest changes the bread and wine into the Body and Blood of Christ. The two consecrations are separated to represent the death of Jesus when he shed all his blood for our salvation. This is the unbloody sacrifice described and defined by the Council of Trent in the 16th century. The priest recites prayers which beg Christ to bless all of us, to forgive our sins, and to give us his grace of eternal life. This part is concluded with the solemn prayer: "Through Him, and with Him, and in Him, be unto Thee, O God the Father almighty, in the unity of the Holy Spirit, all honor and glory, world without end. Amen" (*Per ipsum et cum ipso et in ipso....*). (3) Communion. Next comes the Communion which is introduced by the *Our Father.* In the Communion Christ comes to us in his substantial, Real Presence, under the appearance of bread and wine. The Post-communion prayer concludes this part of the Mass. (4) Conclusion. The conclusion of the Mass is brief: the priest faces the people and says "*Ite missa est,*" that is, "Go, the Mass is ended." Then he gives the people a final blessing, and reads the Last Gospel of St. John. The priest then kneels before the altar and leads the people is saying the Leonine Prayers. After that he dons his biretta and slowly exits the sanctuary.

II. Explanation of the Mass

There is an essential connection between the Mass we celebrate today and the bloody, sacrificial death of Jesus on Calvary in Jerusalem 2000 years ago. It is important to remember that with God there is no time – he is outside of time and all time since the beginning of creation is always present before him. The Mass can be briefly defined as: "The unbloody presence of the unique bloody sacrifice of the cross." So the Mass and Calvary are the same sacrifice, only the mode of offering is different: on the cross it was bloody and brutal, in the Mass it is unbloody, sacramental and peaceful.

It is important to understand and remember that the

Mass is not a different sacrifice from that of Calvary – it is the exact same sacrifice, only the mode of presence is different. The presence of the glorified Jesus after the consecration under the species of bread and wine is called "substantial." There is also an operative presence of Jesus in the sense that his grace is applied to those who take part in the Mass.

In a true sacrifice there is a priest and a victim. On Calvary, Jesus was both priest and victim – he offered himself to the Father for our salvation. In the Mass Jesus is the priest and the victim, operating through the human priest and offering himself to the Father for us.

The heart of the Mass, the essential part, is the consecration of the bread and wine into the Body and Blood of Christ. It is clear that the priest acts "in the person of Christ" because he says, using the first person: "This is MY body" and "This is the cup of MY blood."

Let me remind you again that the Mass is not a repetition of Calvary; it is not a renewal of Calvary – it is rather making the unique sacrifice of Calvary now present on the altar. The same sacrifice, only in an unbloody way. How is this done? It is done by the almighty power of God – it is a miracle. That is why it is called a "mystery of faith" (Latin: *Mysterium fidei*).

The consecration which makes Christ present on the altar is more important than the reception of Communion. This should be obvious since we are commanded by the Church to attend Mass on Sundays and Holy Days, but we are not required to receive Communion at every Mass.

The miraculous change of bread and wine into the Body and Blood of Christ is called by the Church "transubstantiation." This means that the substance of the bread and wine is changed by the creative power of God into the substance of the Body and Blood of Christ. This means that, after the consecration, the bread and wine are no longer bread and wine, even though they appear to our senses to be that. The reality is the Body and Blood of Christ under the appearances of bread and wine. To believe this requires faith and that is why it is called a "Mystery of Faith."

Over the centuries the Mass has had different names, such as Breaking of Bread, Eucharist, and Liturgy.

Conclusion

We should thank God from the bottom of our hearts for the Holy Sacrifice of the Mass. It is the heart of our Catholic faith. The purpose of the Mass is fourfold: Adoration of God, Thanksgiving, Petition and Satisfaction.

The fruits of the Mass are many: (1) General Fruit means the grace from the Mass for all the members of the Church, since the grace of Christ is infinite; (2) Special Fruit means the grace given to those for whom the Mass if offered; (3) Personal Fruit means the grace the priest receives for offering the Mass and the grace the people receive who attend the Mass.

In the Mass Jesus offers himself to the Father. To gain abundant spiritual fruit from the Masses we attend we should offer ourselves with Jesus Christ to the Father. I hope this brief explanation of the Holy Sacrifice of the Mass will help you to better understand what takes place at every Mass and help you to participate in the Mass in a more active manner. God bless you.